★ EVERY DAY EASY ★
AIR FRYER

★ EVERY DAY EASY ★
AIR FRYER
100 RECIPES BURSTING WITH FLAVOR

URVASHI PITRE

Photography by Ghazalle Badiozamani

HOUGHTON MIFFLIN HARCOURT

BOSTON   NEW YORK   2018

For information about permission to reproduce selections from
this book, write to trade.permissions@hmhco.com or to Permissions,
Houghton Mifflin Harcourt Publishing Company, 3 Park Avenue, 19th Floor,
New York, New York 10016.

hmhco.com

Library of Congress Cataloging-in-Publication Data is available.

ISBN 978-1-328-57787-0 (pbk)

ISBN 978-1-328-57609-5 (ebk)

Book design by Jennifer Beal Davis

Printed in the United States of America

DOC 10 9 8 7 6 5 4 3 2 1

To my family, for their unwavering support and love

CONTENTS

ACKNOWLEDGMENTS

I am an open book, yet many people who have known me over the years had no idea I could cook. I spent so much of my time focused on my career that cooking took a back seat to being a busy, career-driven single mother who wanted to do the best for her children.

These same people however have not hesitated to encourage and support me as I started to write recipes, run a blog, and write cookbooks.

I cannot say enough about my husband, Roger, and my sons, Alex and Mark. I am a lucky woman to have them in my life. They are, indeed, my life.

I couldn't have accomplished this book without help from my friend John Kasinger, who meticulously tested the recipes with me, and my friend Diane, who helped in this endeavor, often by tasting and suggesting changes to the recipe. Lisa Kingsley was also of great help as I tried to create recipes for the air fryer that were easy, but yet flavorful.

To my agent, Stacey Glick, thank you so much for helping me navigate my way through the unknown waters. I hope we get to do this together a few dozen more times—at least.

To my editor, Justin Schwartz, the superhero responsible for how fast we put this book together without compromising the quality of the work—it's been fun getting to know you, and to learn from you. I hope we continue down this new path together in the future as well.

Photographer Ghazalle Badiozamani and her team of accomplished stylists and helpers make my food look pretty—not just tasty. Thank you to Monica Pierini, Leila Clifford, Jenna Tedesco, and Bridget Kenny for your great work. Thank you also to Monica and Leila for letting me watch and learn from you.

Thanks also to the whole army at Houghton Mifflin Harcourt that helped without my even realizing it to make this book a reality.

Above all though, I thank my fans, followers and readers. How many bloggers and writers are lucky enough to have a group like you? You, who encourage me to try new things, who are supportive, appreciative, and willing to test and try new things—and completely accepting and supportive of my need to master the next gadget. One day I said I wanted to do an air-fryer cookbook—the next day many of you went out and bought one. Many of the rest of you "slackers" followed mere weeks later. As I experimented and learned, you learned with me and cheered me on. It has been so much fun to do this book with you guys. Thank you for all you do for me, and with me. Here's to many more!

INTRODUCTION

So you bought yourself that air fryer you've been craving. You've made the obvious things like French fries and breaded foods, and every convenience food you thought would work in the air fryer.

Now what?

Well, now you're about to learn that your air fryer is good for more than just breaded and packaged foods. You're about to see how you can start with fresh ingredients and make delicious, healthy dishes with very little work.

I've tried to create dishes that mostly require about ten minutes of prep, a little time to marinate, and just ten to twenty minutes of actual cook time, most of which is unsupervised. Cakes and frittatas are an exception in that they require longer to cook, but the majority of the main dishes come together with very little effort.

Some of you may look at a few of the ingredients and spices and wonder if you really want to get into cooking Indian, Korean, or Sichuan food at home. Here's what I

can tell you: First, yes, you do indeed want to make these simple, flavorful, authentic recipes at home. You can do this. If you can measure, slice, chop, blend, and stir, you can make these recipes. Second, with an air fryer, as with much of cooking, success is all about the spices, marinades, and sauces you use. There are only so many ways you can air-fry plain grilled chicken before you tire of it. After that, your air fryer gets less and less of your attention, and soon you've moved on to the next appliance.

Now, I'm all about the next appliance (#GadgetGeek), but if you follow my advice, you'll find your air fryer is an endless source of varied tastes, a key to using food to open the doors of multiple cultures, and a great way to introduce you and your loved ones to an explosion of flavors.

I've tried to use unusual ingredients in more than one recipe so you have a few different ways to use them. So don't be afraid to buy a few ingredients that seem new and different and give them a whirl. (If you can buy them in smaller quantities, like in the bulk spices section of your grocery store, that's perfect.)

I hope you enjoy each of the well-tested recipes in this book. But most important, I hope this book equips you with the know-how to make your own tweaks and, ultimately, as you get more comfortable with your air fryer, to feel confident making your own air-fryer recipes to enjoy and share.

In fact, my TwoSleevers International Recipes group on Facebook (https://www.facebook.com/groups/twosleevers/) and my blog (www.twosleevers.com) are great places for you to come share your food photos, your questions, and your recipe creations. I hope to see you there!

A FEW WORDS
ABOUT THE RECIPES

EASY

All the recipes in this book are easy enough that novice cooks can make them, but are so flavorful that even experienced cooks will be proud to serve them. If you can chop, mix, and stir, you can make the recipes in this book.

AUTHENTIC

I often use nontraditional techniques, but I strive for authenticity and ease in all recipes. These recipes were taste-tested by people familiar with the cooking of the various countries represented. Only those that were deemed authentic-tasting were included.

TESTED

If you've followed my blog or are in my Face-book group, you know how much I test and retest recipes. Every recipe in this book was tested. If it doesn't work, it's time to trouble-shoot other issues (see page xxiv), because it was likely something other than the recipe that failed you.

FRESH FOODS

I prefer to use fresh ingredients rather than prepackaged foods, so much so that this book includes recipes for making your own spice blends. If I use a prepackaged ingredient (e.g., phyllo dough or puff pastry), it's because that ingredient is truly compli-cated for a home cook to make, and because the store-bought equivalent is of good quality. I also do this when ingredients are not easily found (e.g., myriad ingredients in an authentic Thai Curry Paste). I use canned tomatoes to provide consistency of flavor and canned coconut milk for ease of use. Other than that, it's mainly fresh meats and vegetables!

MOSTLY HANDS OFF

I absolutely detest recipes that require multiple steps, dirty every dish in the house, and call for three appliances—all so you can have a grilled cheese sandwich. The recipes in this book require minimal prep, may only ask you to flip the food once halfway through cooking, if that, and are almost entirely cooked in the air fryer. If you are mobility impaired, have a fractious child who needs to be held, or would rather check your phone than babysit your food, you will appreciate the ease of the recipes in this book.

NO PREHEATING REQUIRED

I have a confession to make. Never in my years of cooking have I ever preheated an oven for a recipe. And yet somehow, I have managed to survive and thrive. None of the recipes in this book call for preheating. In addition to my #ruthlessefficiency approach to cooking, this is in part due to the fact that not all air fryers are equipped for timed preheating. The cook times specified assume you're starting with a cold air fryer.

REQUIRE MINIMAL TWEAKING

I tested these recipes in a GoWISE 3.7-quart air fryer and a Philips Avance Airfryer XL, which have very different price points and also differ in wattage. By and large, however, the cook times required for both were quite consistent. Since other air fryers may differ in wattage and capacity, the first few times you make a recipe from this book, I'd suggest you check the food a few minutes before the end of the cooking time, just in case your air fryer is "special."

HOW IS AN AIR FRYER DIFFERENT FROM AN OVEN?

This question comes up a lot. What's the difference between an air fryer, a regular (conduction) oven, and a convection oven? Do you really need all three? An air fryer is mostly a self-contained convection oven with a powerful fan. What differentiates it from a regular oven is that it uses convection rather than conduction to heat food. What differentiates it from a convection oven can be the intensity of the forced fan heat. Here's a quick primer on conduction ovens, convection ovens, and air fryers, and why I like having my air fryer in addition to my oven.

CONDUCTION VS. CONVECTION

Conduction cooking is when cold food heats up via direct contact with a hotter surface or other hot food. You put a pan on the stove. The stove heats the pan. The pan heats the food. You get to eat dinner. This is direct heat transfer from one object to another. Heat flows from a hot object/surface to a colder object/surface. With convection cooking, not only do you have this type of direct transfer, you have one additional source of heat: hot air. A fan in the oven circulates hot air around the food, resulting in more even cooking. I know you want to make jokes here (or maybe that's just me), but this hot air circulating in the oven touches the surface of the food in the oven, and cooks, or "air-fries" the food, resulting in a crisp outer crust. In this case, it is the hot molecules of air that are also cooking your food, not just heat transfer from one object to another.

WHY DOES ANY OF THIS MATTER TO A COOK?

The main reason these things matter is because with convection cooking the circulating hot air is capable of creating a crust of crispiness on the outside of food, which is something we typically associate with fried food.

The air in a traditional oven, which is mostly just hanging around, not circulating, can also get humid and create a moist environment. The fan in a convection oven ensures that the air stays relatively dry, once again helping to create crispiness on the outside surfaces of foods while the insides stay moist.

CONVECTION OVENS VS. AIR FRYERS

There are four main differences between a convection oven and an air fryer:

1. **The intensity of the fan.** Depending on your convection oven, it may or may not have as powerful a fan to circulate hot air as an air fryer does. This will affect the crispness of the crust, as explained above.

2. **The size of the oven.** Air fryers are smaller, heat up faster, clean up faster, and may brown and crisp foods better due to their smaller size.

3. **Gentler air circulation for baking.** In a convection oven, the fan-forced air can cause delicate baked goods, such as cakes, to collapse. In an air fryer, the fan is typically at the top and is pulling hot air upward, not creating a tempest of hot air everywhere. I've found that cakes actually bake quite well in the air fryer. Sometimes the fan in your air fryer can leave a brown swirl on top of cakes and cause them to cook unevenly. To counteract this, the recipes in this book ask you to cover pans of cake batter with foil before baking.

4. **The smaller capacity of an air-fryer.** Needless to say, smaller air fryers can't hold as much food as a full-size convection oven. If you tend to make a lot of food at a time, your choices are to stick with a full-size oven, buy an air fryer shaped more like a toaster oven (which will have a larger capacity than an egg-shaped fryer), or cook in batches.

So, do you need both? Many people do have both and report that their air fryer produces much crisper food than their convection oven. My suggestion is to start using your convection oven with these recipes and see how you like the way your food turns out. If you are enjoying the recipes, and if you have enough space to house an air fryer, then you may want to add that to your arsenal of kitchen gadgets.

WHY AIR FRY?

HEALTH BENEFITS

The most significant benefit to the air fryer is that it doesn't use nearly the amount of oil as with deep-frying. Most recipes in this book call for 1 to 2 tablespoons of oil per pound of meat or 4 cups of vegetables. Depending on the cut of meat you use, you may not need to add any oil at all.

AIR FRYERS COOK FASTER

To be precise, 20 to 25 percent faster. They also require less energy, as you would typically set your cooking temperatures between 25° and 50°F lower than you would an oven. Additionally, most air fryers preheat in 3 to 5 minutes versus the 20 to 30 minutes an oven needs. Note that since not all air fryers have a preheat setting, the recipes in this book do not call for preheating. Just place your food in the air fryer basket, turn on the time and temperature called for, and walk away.

SAFE AND EASY TO USE

If you're really clumsy, like I am, the thought of being around a pot of hot oil is enough to make you break into a cold sweat. The thought of younger family members trying to fry things unsupervised is even more frightening. Air fryers remove these fears entirely.

Typically, air fryers stay cool to the touch on the outside. The air fryer basket itself does get hot, and I did singe myself a little a time or two as I was testing recipes, but I still think they're a much safer way for youngsters to learn how to cook than hot stoves, hot oil fryers, or even larger ovens.

EASY TO CLEAN

This, to me, is the clear advantage of air fryers over a full-size convection oven. Most of the parts of the air fryer that come into contact with food are dishwasher-safe. I usually wipe the excess oil and crumbs off the basket with a paper towel, run it under hot water briefly, then place it in the dishwasher for a quick clean.

AIR FRYER MYTHS AND REALITIES

MYTH: You don't need to use any oil. Yeah, don't believe that. Use the oil called for in the recipes. Keep a spritzer bottle of oil handy and mist the surfaces if the recipe calls for it. It's worth it to get a crispier outer crust.

MYTH: Odors are contained. Not entirely true. I read a lot about how the fan helps contain odors, etc., but I didn't find this to be true. Reduced odors, perhaps, but not entirely odor-free. I prefer to enjoy the altogether sensual experience of cooking, including the wonderful wafting aromas that serve to tickle your appetite.

MYTH: You don't need to shake up or flip foods. I've read what you have about fan-forced heat obviating the need to shake or flip your food. Ignore that. If a recipe asks you to shake or flip the food, do it. I tested recipes both ways and found that even with the most expensive air fryers, flipping the food resulted in a much more even and crispier crust than if I skipped this step.

MYTH: Your food tastes fried. Well, let's just say "fried-ish." No one is going to mistake that air-fried potato chip for a deep-fried potato chip, but that doesn't mean it isn't delicious.

MYTH: You can make anything taste good in an air fryer. Foods that are naturally fattier do much better than lean foods. A well-marbled pork shoulder will be crispier, moister, and juicier when cooked in the air fryer than a lean pork tenderloin will. I have been careful to specify the cut of meat in each recipe. Feel free to adjust to suit your tastes, but be prepared for the food to taste different. If you pick the right ingredients and add oil or water as called for in the recipe, you can make delicious meals in your air fryer.

REALITY: Your food tastes different than if you'd baked it. It really does. The crispier outer crust air-frying produces does make your food taste different than if you'd merely baked it.

REALITY: Foods come out of the air fryer crisp and crunchy. Most food is indeed crisp and crunchy. This is primarily because of the airflow and drier air in the appliance, and because the air fryer can toast and dehydrate faster than a regular oven can. So much so that at first, you may want to keep an eye on your food as it nears the end of its cook time to ensure it doesn't get overly crunchy (which is my nice way of saying "burnt").

REALITY: Food cooks faster. True, it does cook faster, and at a much lower temperature. If you're making convenience foods from a package (hey, I'm not judging!), you should reduce both the time and the temperature indicated on the package to get good results.

REALITY: You won't heat up the kitchen. If you live in a hot climate, you'll really appreciate this feature as much as I do! The ability to have a cool kitchen while happily baking a cake is reason enough to own an air fryer. I also find it useful when your larger oven is occupied, as it serves nicely as a backup oven for reheating foods and cooking entire dishes.

HELPFUL ACCESSORIES

Heat-Safe Baking Pan

I tried to use only a 7-inch round baking pan for any recipes that needed a pan, so that you wouldn't have to have multiple pans. This pan fits in a 3.7-quart air fryer as well as it fit into a 5-quart-plus air fryer, which allows me to specify uniform cooking times. Be aware that if you use a glass pan, you may have to tweak times and temperatures.

Trivet/Rack

Despite what you've read, I found it was really important to only have one layer of food in the basket. Any more than that, and the top layer would cook—indeed, even overcook—while the middle stayed raw. If you want to double the recipes, you may need to use a rack and place some food in the basket and some on the rack to get even cooking.

Springform or Removable-Bottom Cake Pan

Strictly speaking, this is not a must-have, but it's very nice to have, especially if you want to unmold your cakes and frittatas and pres-

ent them beautifully. You can achieve similar effects by either greasing a cake pan very well or using a parchment paper round at the bottom when making cakes or brownies.

Tongs

I used 7-inch tongs with silicone tips to place food in the air fryer and flip it as I cooked. These are quite handy to have and keep you from tearing up the food as you flip it.

Silicone Oven Mitts

I find these great for lifting out hot pans that may be filled with liquid. They also stow away neatly in a kitchen drawer.

Oil Spritzer or Mister

For best results, you should spray a little oil on the outside of any food that's not inherently fatty. The little spritz of oil really helps with browning and getting a crisp crust. I will be honest—I used PAM coconut oil spray for most of my cooking for this book, largely because I was driven mad by all the self-fill spritzer bottles that only worked twice and then died on me. If you are fortunate enough to have a spray bottle you love, use it. Otherwise, do what I did—buy a spray with propellant and don't worry about it.

For those who have my Instant Pot cookbooks, you will be pleased to know that these are also the accessories I use for my Instant Pot cooking, and that all will fit into a 6-quart Instant Pot. #ruthlessefficiency

TROUBLESHOOTING

It's Taking a Lot Longer Than You Say for My Food to Cook

There could be a few different reasons why this is happening. Once you figure out which it is, it will be an easy fix.

- Your air fryer is a different wattage and/or the fan isn't as powerful as the ones in the air fryers I used for testing (a GoWISE 3.7-quart and a Philips Avance XL).
- Your pieces of meat or vegetables are larger than the recipe calls for. The thickness of the food item can drastically affect cook times.
- You're using a deeper cake pan than specified. The thicker the cake/frittata, the longer it will take to cook.
- You're doubling the recipe. The fuller the basket, the longer it will take to cook the food.

The Food Is Partly Cooked and Partly Raw

This can happen if your food isn't in one layer in the air fryer. If you need to double the recipe, I strongly suggest you do so by cooking in two batches rather than trying to put 2 pounds of meat into the air-fryer basket, which was not intended to hold that much in one go. Since most of the recipes in this cookbook only cook for 10 to 20 minutes, it's as fast to cook two batches as one overfull batch, and your food will cook more evenly.

My Meat Was Dry Even Though I Followed the Recipe (Oh, But I Did Change the Cut of Meat)

Fattier foods cook better in the air fryer than leaner foods. You can cook lean meats in the air fryer, but you may have to spray with oil more often. For poultry, cuts with the skin on will cook better than skinless pieces. Choose alternate cuts of meat with this in mind. You can definitely substitute your favorite cuts but if the result is too dry, you may need to add more oil, mist with water while cooking, or revert to the specified cut.

There's a Lot of Smoke Coming out of the Machine as It Cooks

If you see white smoke, that's typically from the fat that has rendered while cooking. You can either stop and pour out the excess fat, or you can add a little bit of water to the container below the basket so the hot fat isn't sitting directly on the bottom of the hot container.

If you see black smoke, that could be a sign your machine is not functioning as it should. Turn it off, call customer service, and do not use the air fryer until they tell you it's okay to do so.

I Don't Understand Why I Spent So Much Money on My Stove When All I Ever Use Are My Instant Pot and Air Fryer

Yup, the struggle is real. Honestly, once you get more familiar with your air fryer, you'll find that you're choosing it over the stove, the grill, or the oven for faster cooking, and over the microwave for reheating food without drying it out. It takes a little tweaking to learn the right temperatures and times, but once you have that down, it's so easy to use your air fryer, you'll wonder how you ever got by without it.

EGGS & CHEESE

CHILE-CHEESE TOAST

I grew up eating this for a snack. I know you're wondering what kind of kid eats chiles on toast with some cheese for a snack. An Indian kid, that's who. You can totally doctor this up with fancy-schmancy cheese, more spices, or different types of bread, but when I'm craving a taste of home at breakfast, this is what I make. **SERVINGS: 1**

PREP TIME: 5 MINUTES

COOK TIME: 5 MINUTES

TOTAL TIME: 10 MINUTES

COOK TEMPERATURE: 325°F

DIETARY CONSIDERATIONS: EGG-FREE, NUT-FREE, SOY-FREE, VEGETARIAN

2 tablespoons grated Parmesan cheese

2 tablespoons grated mozzarella cheese

2 teaspoons salted butter, at room temperature

10 to 15 thin slices serrano chile or jalapeño

2 slices sourdough bread

½ teaspoon black pepper (optional)

1. In a small bowl, stir together the Parmesan, mozzarella, butter, and chiles. (You want to make a bit of a paste with all this before you spread it on the bread, because if you don't, you'll have airborne shreds of cheese flying around the air fryer.)

2. Spread half the mixture onto one side of each slice of bread. Sprinkle with the pepper, if using. Place the slices cheese-side up in the air-fryer basket. Set the air fryer to 325°F for 5 minutes, or until the cheese has melted and started to brown slightly. Serve immediately.

GRILLED CHEESE SANDWICHES

I make a mean grilled cheese sandwich on the stovetop—or so I thought. One day, out of sheer laziness, I decided to make it in the air fryer rather than stand at the stove watching the grilled cheese cook. Best. Grilled Cheese Sandwich. Ever. No, really, it is. Try it and tell me what you think. **SERVINGS: 2**

PREP TIME: 5 MINUTES

COOK TIME: 8 MINUTES

TOTAL TIME: 13 MINUTES

COOK TEMPERATURE: 350°F

DIETARY CONSIDERATIONS: NUT-FREE, SOY-FREE

2 tablespoons mayonnaise

4 thick slices sourdough bread

4 thick slices Brie cheese

8 slices hot capicola

1. Spread the mayonnaise on one side of each slice of bread. Place 2 slices of bread in the air-fryer basket, mayonnaise-side down. (You want mayonnaise on the outside surfaces of the bread so that it browns the bread and makes it crispy, crunchy, and delicious.)

2. Place the slices of Brie and capicola on the bread and cover with the remaining two slices of bread, mayonnaise-side up.

3. Set the air fryer to 350°F for 8 minutes, or until the cheese has melted. Serve immediately.

VARIATIONS TO TRY:

★ Pesto and provolone
★ Ham and Swiss
★ Sweet mango chutney and sharp cheddar
★ Russian dressing, pastrami, sauerkraut, and Swiss
★ Fig preserves and Brie
★ Marmalade and Camembert
★ Pesto, shredded rotisserie chicken, and Havarti
★ Shredded leftover brisket, barbecue sauce, and Swiss

HARD-COOKED EGGS

There are so many things to love about this recipe, but the thing I love the most is no dirty dishes. No pot with water boiling, no lid for the pot, no babysitting, and no boiled-egg smell. Just drop in your eggs, go do something else for a few minutes, come back, and your eggs are done. What's more, I have to admit that these eggs are even more consistently cooked than eggs cooked in my beloved pressure cooker. Heresy, I know, but also true. **SERVINGS: 6**

COOK TIME: 15 TO 20 MINUTES

TOTAL TIME: 25 TO 30 MINUTES

COOK TEMPERATURE: 250°F

DIETARY CONSIDERATIONS: GRAIN-FREE, GLUTEN-FREE, NUT-FREE, SOY-FREE, DAIRY-FREE, PALEO, VEGETARIAN

6 large eggs

1. Fit a rack into the air-fryer basket. Arrange the eggs on the rack.

2. Set the air fryer to 250°F for 15 minutes for large eggs (20 minutes for extra-large or jumbo eggs).

3. Meanwhile, fill a large bowl with ice and water.

4. At the end of the cooking time, very carefully remove the hot eggs from the rack and place them in the ice bath for 5 minutes. When the eggs are cool to the touch, drain them and store in the refrigerator for up to a week, or peel and eat them right away!

SCOTCH EGGS

Yes, it's a two-step recipe. You have to make the eggs first and then wrap them. But it's so worth it! I've tried to simplify this by forgoing the typical flour–egg–bread crumb coating because what could possibly be wrong with melted cheese as a coating? Gluten-free, low-carb, but, most important, tasty.   **SERVINGS: 4**

PREP TIME: 20 MINUTES

COOK TIME: 15 MINUTES

TOTAL TIME: 35 MINUTES

COOK TEMPERATURE: 400°F

DIETARY CONSIDERATIONS: GRAIN-FREE, GLUTEN-FREE, NUT-FREE, SOY-FREE, LOW-CARB

1 pound bulk pork sausage

2 tablespoons finely chopped fresh parsley

1 tablespoon finely chopped fresh chives

⅛ teaspoon freshly grated nutmeg

⅛ teaspoon kosher salt

⅛ teaspoon black pepper

4 hard-cooked large eggs (page 6), peeled

1 cup shredded Parmesan cheese

Vegetable oil spray

Coarse mustard, for serving

1. In a large bowl, gently mix the sausage, parsley, chives, nutmeg, salt, and pepper until well combined. Shape the mixture into four equal-size patties.

2. Place one egg on each sausage patty and shape the sausage around the egg, covering it completely. Dredge each sausage-covered egg in the shredded cheese to cover completely, pressing lightly to adhere. (Make sure the cheese is well adhered to the meat so shreds of cheese don't end up flying around in the air fryer.)

3. Arrange the Scotch eggs in the air-fryer basket. Spray lightly with vegetable oil spray. Set the air fryer to 400°F for 15 minutes. Halfway through the cooking time, turn eggs and spray again.

4. Serve with mustard.

SPICY GREEK BAKED FETA WITH HONEY (FETA PSITI)

PREP TIME: 5 MINUTES

COOK TIME: 10 MINUTES

TOTAL TIME: 15 MINUTES

COOK TEMPERATURE: 400°F

DIETARY CONSIDERATIONS: EGG-FREE, NUT-FREE, SOY-FREE, VEGETARIAN

Who doesn't like melted cheese, right? This one doesn't melt quite all the way, but the feta softens up just the right amount, so you can dip some simple pita chips into it for a quick appetizer or pair it with a salad for a light lunch. **SERVINGS: 4**

- 1 (8-ounce) block feta cheese
- 2 tablespoons extra-virgin olive oil
- 1 tablespoon red pepper flakes
- 1 tablespoon dried oregano
- 2 tablespoons honey
- Pita chips or wedges of fresh pita bread, for serving

1. Cut the block of feta in half horizontally. Cut each piece in half horizontally to create 4 thin pieces of cheese. Arrange the cheese in 7-inch round baking pan.

2. Drizzle the cheese with the oil, using a basting brush to spread it evenly. Sprinkle with the red pepper flakes and oregano. Drizzle evenly with the honey.

3. Place the dish in the air-fryer basket. Set the air fryer to 400°F for 10 minutes.

4. Transfer to a serving plate. Use the basting brush to spread any oil and honey that have dripped to the bottom of the dish on top of the cheese. Serve with pita chips or fresh pita wedges.

VARIATIONS TO TRY:

Add any of the following before baking the spiced cheese:
- ★ Sliced tomatoes
- ★ Sliced bell peppers
- ★ Pickled Peppadew peppers

JALAPEÑO POPPER BAKE

You can never have too much bacon, nor too much cheese. If your household is like any of the others that have enjoyed this dip, I can tell you that it will disappear in minutes. It's quite substantial, so it needs a good, thick chip or melba toast for scooping—pass on the thin potato chips for this one. Or, you know, a spoon dipped straight into the pan works, too. I'm not judging! **SERVINGS: 8 TO 10**

PREP TIME: 15 MINUTES

COOK TIME: 15 MINUTES

TOTAL TIME: 30 MINUTES

COOK TEMPERATURE: 400°F

DIETARY CONSIDERATIONS:
GRAIN-FREE, GLUTEN-FREE,
EGG-FREE, NUT-FREE,
SOY-FREE, LOW-CARB

Vegetable oil, for greasing

1½ pounds boneless, skinless chicken thighs, diced

½ cup diced bell pepper

1 to 4 jalapeños, minced

2 ounces cream cheese, softened

1 cup shredded Mexican cheese blend

1 teaspoon chili powder

½ teaspoon garlic salt

½ teaspoon kosher salt

4 slices bacon

¼ cup chopped scallions, for garnish

Celery sticks, baby carrots, bell pepper strips, broccoli florets, cauliflower florets, and/or tortilla chips, for serving

---

I. Grease a 7½-inch barrel cake pan (see Note) with oil.

2. In a large bowl, stir together the chicken, bell pepper, jalapeños, cream cheese, Mexican cheese blend, chili powder, garlic salt, and salt until thoroughly combined. Transfer the mixture to the prepared pan.

3. Cut each bacon slice into three or four pieces. Arrange the bacon in a circle on top of the chicken mixture. Place the pan in the air-fryer basket. Set the air fryer to 400°F for 15 minutes, or until the cheese has melted and the chicken is cooked through.

4. Sprinkle with the scallions and serve with vegetables and/or tortilla chips for dipping.

NOTE:

★ This recipe was written to be made in an extra-deep 7½-inch round pan called a barrel pan or cake barrel, which is sold as an accessory for air fryers with a capacity of 5.3 quarts or more. If your fryer is smaller than that, use a 6-inch round cake pan with 4-inch sides and increase the cooking time by 5 to 8 minutes.

FRESH HERB & CHEDDAR FRITTATA

Thanks to Google, I know the difference between an omelet, a frittata, and a quiche. This is technically none of those things, since for a frittata, I should have precooked some of the ingredients. But I'm lazy/efficient. So here you are, an easy one-shot egg casserole that's perfect for brunch. The trick with eggs in an air fryer is to cook them low and slow—high heat just doesn't work for eggs. **SERVINGS: 2**

PREP TIME: 10 MINUTES

COOK TIME: 20 MINUTES

TOTAL TIME: 30 MINUTES

COOK TEMPERATURE: 300°F

DIETARY CONSIDERATIONS: GRAIN-FREE, GLUTEN-FREE, NUT-FREE, SOY-FREE, VEGETARIAN, LOW-CARB

Vegetable oil, for greasing

4 large eggs

½ cup half-and-half

½ cup shredded cheddar cheese

2 tablespoons chopped scallion greens

2 tablespoons chopped fresh parsley or cilantro

½ teaspoon kosher salt

½ teaspoon black pepper

1. Generously grease a 7-inch round baking pan. (Be sure to grease the pan well—the proteins in eggs stick something fierce. Alternatively, line the bottom of the pan with a round of parchment paper cut to fit and spray the parchment and sides of the pan generously with vegetable oil spray.)

2. In a large bowl, beat together the eggs and half-and-half. Stir in the cheese, scallions, parsley, salt, and pepper. Pour the mixture into the prepared pan. Place the pan in the air-fryer basket. Set the air fryer to 300°F for 20 minutes, or until the eggs are set and a toothpick inserted into the center comes out clean.

3. Serve the frittata warm or at room temperature.

CHEESE & VEGGIE EGG CUPS

I can't believe I'm giving you a recipe for something so simple, but I know you'll thank me once you make them. What I love about this is that you can treat it as a basic recipe and mix and match the meat and veggies you add. It also makes great single servings that people can grab and reheat as they like. **SERVINGS: 2**

PREP TIME: 10 MINUTES

COOK TIME: 19 MINUTES

TOTAL TIME: 30 MINUTES

COOK TEMPERATURE:
300°F/400°F

DIETARY CONSIDERATIONS:
GRAIN-FREE, GLUTEN-FREE,
NUT-FREE, SOY-FREE,
VEGETARIAN, LOW-CARB

Vegetable oil,
for greasing

2 large eggs

½ cup mixed diced
vegetables, such
as onions, bell
peppers, mushrooms,
tomatoes

½ cup shredded sharp
cheddar cheese

2 tablespoons half-and-
half

1 tablespoon chopped
fresh cilantro (or
other fresh herb
of your choice)

Kosher salt and black
pepper

1. Grease two 6-ounce ramekins with vegetable oil.

2. In a medium bowl, whisk together the eggs, vegetables, ¼ cup of the cheese, the half-and-half, cilantro, and salt and pepper to taste. Divide the mixture between the prepared ramekins.

3. Place the ramekins in the air-fryer basket. Set the air fryer to 300°F for 15 minutes.

4. Top the cups with the remaining ¼ cup cheese. Set the air fryer to 400°F and cook for 4 minutes, until the cheese on top is melted and lightly browned.

5. Serve immediately, or store in an airtight container in the refrigerator up to a week.

PHYLLO-WRAPPED BRIE WITH FIG JAM

PREP TIME: 20 MINUTES

COOK TIME: 15 MINUTES

TOTAL TIME: 35 MINUTES

COOK TEMPERATURE: 400°F

DIETARY CONSIDERATIONS: EGG-FREE, NUT-FREE, SOY-FREE, VEGETARIAN

I shouldn't brag about my own recipes, but people, this dish looks like a work of art. It looks crazy elegant for something that uses so few ingredients. The only thing that may be a little tricky is the phyllo. I suggest you plan to make it several times until you get the hang of it, varying the jams, chutneys, and nuts you use until it's just perfect for you. #ForResearch #SacrificeYourself **SERVINGS: 4**

8   sheets frozen phyllo pastry, thawed (see Note)

⅓   cup salted butter, melted

1   (8-ounce) round Brie cheese

2   tablespoons fig jam or cranberry jelly

Apple and/or pear wedges, for serving

1. Place 1 sheet of the phyllo in a 7-inch round baking pan. Press the phyllo sheet to conform to the shape of the pan, leaving the excess overhanging the edges. Brush the phyllo all over with some of the melted butter. Place another sheet of phyllo on top, offsetting the overhanging corners of the sheets so you have some overlap. Brush with some of the melted butter. Continue in this manner until you have used up all 8 sheets, brushing butter between each layer. (Be sure to press the sheets against the sides of the pan—you are using the pan as a mold to get a perfectly rounded pastry.)

2. Use a vegetable peeler to lightly scrape off some of the Brie rind. Place the cheese in the pan in the center of the phyllo sheets. Spread with the fig jam. Carefully fold over the phyllo sheets one layer at a time, starting with the top layer and brushing with butter as you go. Press down so the cheese is well covered, making sure the sheets stick together. Brush with any remaining butter.

3. Place the pan in the air-fryer basket. Set the air fryer to 400°F for 15 minutes, checking at 10 minutes to make sure the phyllo is browning evenly. If it is browning unevenly, rotate the pan a quarter turn in the basket and continue cooking. When the phyllo is browned, the cheese is melted and ready to serve.

4. Serve with apple and/or pear wedges.

NOTE:

★ To prevent the phyllo sheets from drying out as you work, keep them covered with a clean, barely damp kitchen towel.

FRICO (CHEESE CRISPS)

Frico, or cheese chips, as I like to call them, are in the arsenal of every devoted low-carber. But really, they're so tasty that every-one should be eating them all the time. If you have trouble with the cheese flying around, set a sheet of parchment paper on top and place a rack or trivet on the parchment to keep the cheese from flying around.   **SERVINGS: 2**

PREP TIME: 10 MINUTES

COOK TIME: 5 MINUTES

TOTAL TIME: 15 MINUTES

COOK TEMPERATURE: 375°F

DIETARY CONSIDERATIONS:
EGG-FREE, NUT-FREE,
SOY-FREE, VEGETARIAN,
LOW-CARB

1   **cup shredded or grated aged Manchego cheese**

1   **teaspoon all-purpose flour**

½   **teaspoon cumin seeds**

¼   **teaspoon cracked black pepper**

1. Line the air-fryer basket with a round of parchment paper cut to fit.

2. In a small bowl, toss together the cheese and flour. Sprinkle the cheese in a 4 to 4½-inch round in the center of the parchment-lined air-fryer basket. In a small bowl, stir together the cumin seeds and pepper. Sprinkle the spices on top of the cheese.

3. Set the air fryer to 375°F for 5 minutes. After 4 minutes, check for doneness: The cheese should be bubbling and just starting to darken a bit. If not, cook for 1 minute more. Use a thin, flexible metal spatula to transfer the cheese wafer to a paper towel-lined baking sheet to cool (it will continue to crisp up as it cools).

4. While the cheese wafer is still warm, cut it into wedges and let cool completely. Serve the cheese wafers, or store between layers of waxed paper or parchment paper in an airtight container at room temperature for up to 5 days.

VARIATIONS TO TRY:

Substitute the following—use the 1 teaspoon flour for all variations.
- ★ 1 cup finely shredded or grated sharp aged white cheddar, ⅛ teaspoon cayenne pepper, and ¼ teaspoon cracked black pepper
- ★ 1 cup finely shredded or grated Parmesan, ½ teaspoon fennel seeds, 1 teaspoon grated lemon zest, and 2 tablespoons finely chopped fresh basil
- ★ 1 cup finely shredded or grated Asiago cheese, 1 tablespoon finely chopped fresh sage, and 2 tablespoons chopped pine nuts
- ★ 1 cup finely shredded or grated aged Gouda cheese, ¼ teaspoon Aleppo pepper or red pepper flakes, 2 teaspoons fresh thyme leaves, and 2 tablespoons chopped pecans

PUFF PASTRY BITES WITH GOAT CHEESE, FIGS & PROSCIUTTO

PREP TIME: 30 MINUTES

COOK TIME: 10 MINUTES (PER BATCH)

TOTAL TIME: 50 MINUTES

COOK TEMPERATURE: 400°F

DIETARY CONSIDERATIONS: NUT-FREE, SOY-FREE

This one is a great recipe for unexpected company. As long as you have a package of puff pastry, you can make up these little appetizers in a jiffy. If you vary this up, be sure to include a combination of creamy cheese, sweet fruit, and something a little salty so you have a great mix of flavors.

SERVINGS: 8 (2 PASTRIES EACH)

2   slices prosciutto

½   cup soft goat cheese

4   dried Mission figs, chopped

2   teaspoons snipped fresh tarragon or basil

1   large egg

1   tablespoon water

    All-purpose flour

1   sheet frozen puff pastry (from a 17.3-ounce package), thawed

1. Place the prosciutto slices on a paper towel. Lay another towel on top. Microwave on high for 1 minute. Remove the top paper towel and let cool completely (the meat will be slightly flexible but will crisp up as it cools). Crumble the prosciutto; set aside.

2. In a medium bowl, stir together the goat cheese, figs, crisped prosciutto, and tarragon until well blended.

3. In a small bowl, beat the egg and water with a fork to make an egg wash. Lightly flour a work surface. Roll out the thawed puff pastry sheet to a 12-inch square. Using a pizza cutter, cut the pastry into sixteen 3-inch squares. Brush the edges of the squares with the egg wash.

4. Place about 2 teaspoons of the goat cheese mixture in the center of each square. Fold the pastry over the filling to form triangles, pressing the edges to seal. Crimp the edges with a fork.

5. Arrange 8 of the pastry triangles in the air-fryer basket, leaving as much space as possible between them. Set the air fryer to 400°F for 10 minutes, or until the pastry is golden brown. Transfer the finished pastries to a serving plate and repeat with the remaining pastry triangles.

6. Serve warm.

PANEER TIKKA BITES

If you've never made paneer before, you can look up the simple recipe for it on my blog, TwoSleevers.com, but you might be able to buy frozen paneer from your local Indian grocery store. Paneer is perfect for the air fryer since it softens with heat but doesn't melt, leaving the little pillows of spiced goodness intact. Put festive toothpicks in each one and watch them disappear. **SERVINGS: 4**

PREP TIME: 10 MINUTES

MARINATING TIME: 30 MINUTES

COOK TIME: 10 MINUTES

TOTAL TIME: 50 MINUTES

COOK TEMPERATURE: 325°F

DIETARY CONSIDERATIONS: GRAIN-FREE, GLUTEN-FREE, EGG-FREE, NUT-FREE, SOY-FREE, VEGETARIAN, LOW-CARB

2 cups cubed paneer cheese

1 tablespoon vegetable oil or melted ghee (page 187)

1 teaspoon minced garlic

1 teaspoon minced fresh ginger

1 teaspoon kosher salt

1 teaspoon Garam Masala (page 181)

½ teaspoon ground turmeric

½ teaspoon smoked paprika

¼ teaspoon ground cumin

¼ teaspoon ground coriander

¼ teaspoon cayenne pepper

1 tablespoon fresh lemon juice

¼ cup chopped fresh cilantro or parsley

1. In a large bowl, combine the cheese, oil, garlic, ginger, salt, garam masala, turmeric, paprika, cumin, coriander, and cayenne. Using your hands, gently mix everything together, taking care not to break up the cheese. Marinate for 30 minutes at room temperature or cover and refrigerate for up to 24 hours.

2. Place the cheese in a single layer in the air-fryer basket. Set the air fryer to 325°F for 10 minutes, turning the cubes halfway through the cooking time.

3. Transfer the paneer to a serving plate and drizzle with the lemon juice. Toss to combine. Sprinkle with the cilantro and serve immediately.

HALLOUMI WITH GREEK SALSA

PREP TIME: 15 MINUTES

COOK TIME: 6 MINUTES

TOTAL TIME: 21 MINUTES

COOK TEMPERATURE: 375°F

DIETARY CONSIDERATIONS: GRAIN-FREE, GLUTEN-FREE, EGG-FREE, NUT-FREE, SOY-FREE, VEGETARIAN, LOW-CARB

Yes, I know there's no such thing as a Greek salsa—or I should say, there was no such thing, because once you taste this mix of veggies and herbs, you'll agree with me that there should have been one all along. Light, refreshing salsa with creamy cheese—hard to beat that combination! **SERVINGS: 4**

For the Salsa

1 small shallot, fincly diced

3 garlic cloves, minced

2 tablespoons fresh lemon juice

2 tablespoons extra-virgin olive oil

1 teaspoon freshly cracked black pepper

Pinch of kosher salt

½ cup finely diced English cucumber

1 plum tomato, seeded and finely diced

2 teaspoons chopped fresh parsley

1 teaspoon snipped fresh dill

1 teaspoon snipped fresh oregano

For the Cheese

8 ounces halloumi cheese, sliced into ½-inch-thick pieces

1 tablespoon extra-virgin olive oil

1. **For the salsa:** Combine the shallot, garlic, lemon juice, olive oil, pepper, and salt in a medium bowl. Add the cucumber, tomato, parsley, dill, and oregano. Toss gently to combine; set aside.

2. **For the cheese:** Place the cheese slices in a medium bowl. Drizzle with the olive oil. Toss gently to coat. Arrange the cheese in a single layer in the air-fryer basket. Set the air fryer to 375°F for 6 minutes.

3. Divide the cheese among four serving plates. Top with the salsa and serve immediately.

BBQ CHICKEN FLATBREADS

I love simple recipes that you can put together with pantry ingredients. But I also love recipes where each family member can customize their serving, and these flatbreads certainly allow you to do that. I'd suggest setting up a pizza bar and letting everyone make their own—which is a nice way to get the night off from cooking, too!

SERVINGS: 2 TO 4

PREP TIME: 10 MINUTES

COOK TIME: 10 MINUTES

TOTAL TIME: 20 MINUTES

COOK TEMPERATURE: 400°F

DIETARY CONSIDERATIONS: EGG-FREE, NUT-FREE, SOY-FREE

2 cups chopped cooked chicken

¾ cup prepared barbecue sauce

2 prepared naan flatbreads

½ cup shredded smoked Gouda cheese

¾ cup shredded mozzarella cheese

½ small red onion, halved and thinly sliced

2 tablespoons chopped fresh cilantro

1. In a medium bowl, toss together the chicken and ¼ cup of the barbecue sauce.

2. Spread half the remaining barbecue sauce on one of the flat-breads. Top with half the chicken and half each of the Gouda and mozzarella cheeses. Sprinkle with half the red onion. Gently press the cheese and onions onto the chicken with your fingers.

3. Carefully place one flatbread in the air-fryer basket. Set the air fryer to 400°F for 10 minutes, until the bread is browned around the edges and the cheese is bubbling and golden brown. If not, cook for 2 minutes more. Transfer the flatbread to a plate and repeat to cook the second flatbread.

4. Sprinkle with the chopped cilantro before serving.

recipe continues →

VARIATIONS

GREEK CHICKEN FLATBREADS

Stir together 2 tablespoons extra-virgin olive oil and 1 teaspoon minced fresh garlic. Brush 2 naan flatbreads with the garlic oil. Top each with 1 cup chopped cooked chicken, ¼ cup diced seeded plum tomato, ⅓ cup chopped artichoke hearts, ¼ cup halved Kalamata olives, and ⅓ cup crumbled feta cheese. Follow the cooking directions for BBQ Chicken Flatbreads. Sprinkle each flatbread with ¼ teaspoon dried oregano and 1 tablespoon chopped fresh flat-leaf parsley before serving.

THAI CHICKEN FLATBREADS

Make a double batch of the Easy Peanut Sauce on page 185. In a medium bowl, toss together 2 cups chopped cooked chicken and ¼ cup of the peanut sauce. Spread ¼ cup of the peanut sauce on 1 naan flatbread. Top with half the chicken, ¼ cup shredded carrot, ⅓ cup bean sprouts, and ½ cup shredded mozzarella. Gently press the cheese and vegetables onto the chicken with your fingers. Follow the cooking directions for BBQ Chicken Flatbreads. Repeat to make a second flatbread. Sprinkle each flatbread with 1 tablespoon chopped fresh cilantro, 1 tablespoon chopped roasted peanuts, and red pepper flakes to taste before serving.

BUFFALO CHICKEN FLATBREADS

In a small saucepan, combine ½ cup Buffalo sauce, 2 tablespoons salted butter, and ¼ teaspoon black pepper. Heat over medium-low heat until the butter has melted. Whisk to combine. Toss 2 cups chopped cooked chicken with 2 tablespoons of the sauce.

Spread 2 naan flatbreads with the remaining sauce. Top each with half the chicken, ½ cup shredded Monterey Jack cheese, and 2 tablespoons crumbled blue cheese. Gently press the cheese onto the chicken with your fingers. Follow the cooking directions for BBQ Chicken Flatbreads. Sprinkle each flatbread with 1 tablespoon thinly sliced scallions before serving.

PESTO CHICKEN FLATBREADS

In a medium bowl, toss together 2 cups chopped cooked chicken and 2 tablespoons Quick Basil Pesto (recipe follows). Spread 2 naan flatbreads with 1 tablespoon of the pesto each. Top each flatbread with half the chicken and ¾ cup shredded Asiago cheese. Gently press the cheese onto the chicken with your fingers. Follow the cooking directions for BBQ Chicken Flatbreads. Top each flatbread with ½ cup fresh arugula, squeeze a lemon wedge over each, and drizzle with extra-virgin olive oil before serving.

QUICK BASIL PESTO

In a blender or food processor, combine 1½ cups packed fresh basil leaves; ½ cup grated Parmesan or Pecorino Romano cheese; ¼ cup pine nuts, walnuts, or almonds; 1 garlic clove, coarsely chopped; and ¼ teaspoon kosher salt. Pulse until a paste forms, stopping occasionally to scrape down the sides. With the motor running, gradually drizzle in ¼ cup extra-virgin olive oil. Refrigerate any unused pesto in an airtight container for 1 to 2 days or freeze for up to 1 month.

HOT CRAB DIP

Here's another substantial cheesy dip that, when combined with Melba toast or crudités, a little salad, and a glass of wine, could make a light supper for a stay-home date night (which means we can wear pajamas on our date, right?). There's a bit of spice in this recipe, so vary the amount of hot sauce to suit your tastes. **SERVINGS: 4**

PREP TIME: 5 MINUTES

COOK TIME: 7 MINUTES

TOTAL TIME: 12 MINUTES

COOK TEMPERATURE: 400°F

DIETARY CONSIDERATIONS: GRAIN-FREE, GLUTEN-FREE, NUT-FREE, SOY-FREE, LOW-CARB

1 cup lump crabmeat

¼ cup mayonnaise

2 cups shredded pepper Jack cheese

½ cup sliced scallions

2 tablespoons hot sauce

½ teaspoon kosher salt

1 teaspoon black pepper

2 tablespoons fresh lemon juice

2 tablespoons chopped fresh parsley

Celery sticks, carrot sticks, and bell pepper strips, or Melba toast for dipping

1. In a 7-inch round baking pan, stir together the crab, mayonnaise, cheese, scallions, hot sauce, salt, and pepper until thoroughly combined.

2. Place the pan in the air-fryer basket. Set the air fryer to 400°F for 7 minutes, or until the cheese is melted and the top is lightly golden brown.

3. Stir in the lemon juice and parsley

4. Serve hot, with vegetables for dipping.

CREAM CHEESE WONTONS

These little wontons are super versatile because you can combine them with either a sweet preserve or a savory chutney. But really, it's hard to go wrong with a crispy wonton, filled with sweet, melted cream cheese. I know I say you should make four wontons for each serving, but I'll be the first to admit that four may not be nearly enough. The only trick to these is to only use ¼ to ½ teaspoon of filling in each, so that they don't burst open while cooking. If they do burst open, resist the urge to lick that cheese. It's very hot and clingy (kinda like your ex, and equally likely to burn you).

SERVINGS: 4

PREP TIME: 10 MINUTES

COOK TIME: 6 MINUTES

TOTAL TIME: 16 MINUTES

COOK TEMPERATURE: 350°F

DIETARY CONSIDERATIONS: EGG-FREE, NUT-FREE, SOY-FREE, VEGETARIAN

2 ounces cream cheese

1 tablespoon sugar

16 square wonton wrappers

Vegetable oil spray

¼ cup jam or chutney, for dipping

1. Place the cream cheese in a microwave-safe bowl and microwave on high for 30 seconds to soften. Add the sugar and stir until well combined.

2. Fill a small bowl of water and set it next to you. Place a generous ¼ teaspoon of cream cheese in a wonton wrapper. Wet your index finger in the bowl of water and run it over the edges of the wrapper. Fold over the wrapper into a triangle. Wet the two longer edges and fold over to make an envelope shape. Place the wonton, standing up, in the air-fryer basket. Repeat with the remaining wonton wrappers and cream cheese mixture.

3. Spray the wontons with vegetable oil spray. Set the air fryer to 350°F for 6 minutes.

4. Serve with jam or chutney.

VEGETABLES

TART & SPICY INDIAN POTATOES (AMCHOOR POTATOES)

PREP TIME: 10 MINUTES

COOK TIME: 15 MINUTES

TOTAL TIME: 25 MINUTES

COOK TEMPERATURE: 400°F

DIETARY CONSIDERATIONS:
GRAIN-FREE, GLUTEN-FREE,
EGG-FREE, NUT-FREE,
SOY-FREE, DAIRY-FREE,
VEGAN, VEGETARIAN

I grew up eating these creamy, spicy, tart, and—let's face it—oily potatoes. They are a Punjabi specialty that you'd probably only get in people's houses—and of course, now in your house. Amchoor is made from drying and grinding green mangoes and is used widely for different dishes. You can find it in Indian grocery stores. But you can always substitute a tablespoon or two of lemon juice or lime juice and give that a shot.   **SERVINGS: 4**

4   cups quartered baby yellow potatoes

3   tablespoons vegetable oil

1   teaspoon ground turmeric

1   teaspoon amchoor (see headnote)

1   teaspoon kosher salt

¼   teaspoon ground cumin

¼   teaspoon ground coriander

¼ to ½   teaspoon cayenne pepper

1   tablespoon fresh lime or lemon juice

¼   cup chopped fresh cilantro or parsley

1. In a large bowl, toss together the potatoes, vegetable oil, turmeric, amchoor, salt, cumin, coriander, and cayenne until the potatoes are well coated.

2. Place the seasoned potatoes in the air-fryer basket. Set the air fryer to 400°F for 15 minutes, or until they are cooked through and tender when pierced with a fork.

3. Transfer the potatoes to a serving platter or bowl. Drizzle with the lime juice and sprinkle with the cilantro before serving.

CHILES RELLENOS WITH RED CHILE SAUCE

I love chiles rellenos, but I hate frying. I mean hate it. I haven't fried a thing in my house in thirty years. The air fryer makes recipes like this so easy. I've skipped the batter for this recipe, but it is so full of fresh flavors, you won't miss it. Absolutely do not skip making the red sauce. I rarely give you recipes with multiple steps unless it's truly worth that extra step, and this sauce is utterly worth it. **SERVINGS: 2**

PREP TIME: 20 MINUTES

COOK TIME: 20 MINUTES

TOTAL TIME: 40 MINUTES

COOK TEMPERATURE: 400°F

DIETARY CONSIDERATIONS: GRAIN-FREE, GLUTEN-FREE, EGG-FREE, NUT-FREE, SOY-FREE

For the Peppers

- 2 poblano peppers, rinsed and dried
- ⅔ cup thawed frozen or drained canned corn kernels
- 1 scallion, sliced
- 2 tablespoons chopped fresh cilantro
- ½ teaspoon kosher salt
- ¼ teaspoon black pepper
- ⅔ cup grated Monterey Jack cheese

For the Sauce

- 3 tablespoons extra-virgin olive oil
- ½ cup finely chopped yellow onion
- 2 teaspoons minced garlic
- 1 (6-ounce) can tomato paste

1. **For the peppers:** Place the peppers in the air-fryer basket. Set the air fryer to 400°F for 10 minutes, turning the peppers halfway through the cooking time, until their skins are charred. Transfer the peppers to a resealable plastic bag, seal, and set aside to steam for 5 minutes. Peel the peppers and discard the skins. Cut a slit down the center of each pepper, starting at the stem and continuing to the tip. Remove the seeds, being careful not to tear the chile.

2. In a medium bowl, combine the corn, scallion, cilantro, salt, black pepper, and cheese; set aside.

3. **Meanwhile, for the sauce (see Note):** In a large skillet, heat the olive oil over medium-high heat. Add the onion and cook, stirring, until tender, about 5 minutes. Add the garlic and cook, stirring, for 30 seconds. Stir in the tomato paste, chile powder, oregano, and cumin, and salt. Cook, stirring, for 1 minute. Whisk in the broth and lemon juice. Bring to a simmer and cook, stirring occasionally, while the stuffed peppers finish cooking.

4. Cut a slit down the center of each poblano pepper, starting at the stem and continuing to the tip. Remove the seeds, being careful not to tear the chile.

recipe continues →

2 tablespoons ancho
chile powder

1 teaspoon dried
oregano

1 teaspoon ground
cumin

½ teaspoon kosher salt

2 cups chicken broth

2 tablespoons fresh
lemon juice

Mexican crema
or sour cream,
for serving

5. Carefully stuff each pepper with half the corn mixture. Place the stuffed peppers in a 7-inch round baking pan with 4-inch sides. Place the pan in the air-fryer basket. Set the air fryer to 400°F for 10 minutes, or until the cheese has melted.

6. Transfer the stuffed peppers to a serving platter and drizzle with the sauce and some crema.

NOTE:

★ This recipe makes more sauce than you will use in one meal. Freeze the leftover sauce, and you'll be one step ahead next time you make these chiles rellenos.

MUSHROOMS & BACON

Sometimes as a food blogger/cookbook author, you wonder about giving people something this simple as a recipe. But I'm also a busy mom and wife who likes to cook for her family, and this is an easy, very flavorful dish that I can make without much thought or planning. It's so simple that you could put a younger family member in charge of making it while you get the rest of dinner together. **SERVINGS: 4**

PREP TIME: 5 MINUTES

COOK TIME: 10 MINUTES

TOTAL TIME: 15 MINUTES

COOK TEMPERATURE: 375°F

DIETARY CONSIDERATIONS: GRAIN-FREE, GLUTEN-FREE, EGG-FREE, NUT-FREE, SOY-FREE, DAIRY-FREE, PALEO, LOW-CARB

16 ounces baby bella (cremini) mushrooms, halved

4 slices bacon, each cut into 8 pieces

Kosher salt and black pepper (optional)

¼ cup chopped fresh parsley, for garnish

1. Place the mushrooms in the air-fryer basket. Sprinkle the bacon over the mushrooms. Set the air fryer to 375°F for 10 minutes and cook, very gently shaking the basket halfway through the cooking time—you still want the bacon slices mostly on top. (As the bacon cooks, it drips its luscious fat onto the mushrooms and flavors them with bacon-y goodness.)

2. Taste and season with salt and/or pepper, if necessary; you may not need any.

3. Sprinkle with the parsley and serve.

INDIAN CHINESE CAULIFLOWER (GOBI MANCHURIAN)

PREP TIME: 10 MINUTES

COOK TIME: 20 MINUTES

TOTAL TIME: 30 MINUTES

COOK TEMPERATURE: 400°F

DIETARY CONSIDERATIONS: EGG-FREE, NUT-FREE, DAIRY-FREE, VEGAN, VEGETARIAN, LOW-CARB

Welcome to Chinese food that the Chinese have not even heard of! When the Hakka people migrated to India, they adapted their recipes to work with locally available ingredients. Thus was born Indian Chinese cooking. In the traditional recipe, the cauliflower is battered and deep-fried. But really, most of the taste is in the sauce, not the batter. This version is as tasty, but a lot less greasy than a typical Gobi Manchurian.   **SERVINGS: 4**

For the Cauliflower

- 4 cups chopped cauliflower
- 1 cup chopped yellow onion
- 1 large bell pepper, chopped
- 2 tablespoons vegetable oil
- 2 teaspoons kosher salt
- 1 teaspoon ground turmeric

For the Sauce

- 3 tablespoons ketchup
- 2 tablespoons soy sauce
- 1 tablespoon rice vinegar
- 1 teaspoon minced garlic
- 1 teaspoon minced fresh ginger
- 1 teaspoon sriracha or other hot sauce

1. **For the cauliflower:** In a large bowl, combine the cauliflower, onion, and bell pepper. Drizzle with the vegetable oil and sprinkle with the salt and turmeric. Stir until the cauliflower is well coated.

2. Place the cauliflower in the air-fryer basket. Set the air fryer to 400°F for 20 minutes, stirring the cauliflower halfway through the cooking time.

3. Meanwhile, for the sauce: In a small bowl, combine the ketchup, soy sauce, vinegar, garlic, ginger, and sriracha.

4. Transfer the cauliflower to a large bowl. Pour the sauce over and toss well to combine. Serve immediately.

INDIAN OKRA (BHINDI MASALA)

PREP TIME: 10 MINUTES

COOK TIME: 15 MINUTES

TOTAL TIME: 25 MINUTES

COOK TEMPERATURE: 375°F

DIETARY CONSIDERATIONS:
GRAIN-FREE, GLUTEN-FREE,
EGG-FREE, NUT-FREE,
SOY-FREE, DAIRY-FREE,
VEGAN, VEGETARIAN,
LOW-CARB

Even as a picky child, I could always be counted on to eat okra. That's because the Indian version of okra is almost always a crisp, panfried version. I love that way of eating it, but it uses a lot of oil and it requires near constant stirring. This method of cooking okra is almost effortless, and you get the same crisp taste that you'll soon start to crave.   **SERVINGS: 4**

- About 1 pound okra, sliced ¼ inch thick (4 cups)
- 1 cup coarsely chopped red onion
- 2 tablespoons vegetable oil

- 1 teaspoon ground turmeric
- 1 teaspoon kosher salt
- 1 teaspoon ground cumin
- 1 teaspoon ground coriander
- ¼ to ½ teaspoon cayenne pepper

- ¼ teaspoon amchoor (see page 30; optional)
- ½ cup chopped fresh tomato
- Juice of 1 lemon
- ¼ cup chopped fresh cilantro or parsley

1. In a large bowl, combine the okra and onion. Drizzle with the vegetable oil and sprinkle with the turmeric, salt, cumin, coriander, cayenne, and amchoor (if using).

2. Spread the spiced vegetables over the air-fryer basket, making as even and flat a layer as possible. Set the air fryer to 375°F for 15 minutes, stirring halfway through the cooking time. (Don't panic if you see some stickiness to the okra. This will dissipate once it cooks.) After 10 minutes, add the tomato to the basket. Cook for the remaining 5 minutes, until the tomato is wilted and cooked through.

3. Drizzle the vegetables with the lemon juice and toss to combine. Garnish with the cilantro and serve.

ROASTED CAULIFLOWER WITH TAHINI

PREP TIME: 10 MINUTES

COOK TIME: 20 MINUTES

TOTAL TIME: 30 MINUTES

COOK TEMPERATURE: 400°F

DIETARY CONSIDERATIONS: GRAIN-FREE, GLUTEN-FREE, EGG-FREE, NUT-FREE, SOY-FREE, DAIRY-FREE, VEGAN, VEGETARIAN, LOW-CARB

As if roasted cauliflower weren't delicious enough already, I added tahini, along with a little lemon juice. Can we just say "elevated"? We can. By the way, the twenty-minute cook time is not a typo—cauliflower takes a while to roast in the oven and in the air fryer, so be patient. The results will be worth it.   **SERVINGS: 4**

For the Cauliflower

- 5 cups cauliflower florets (about 1 large head)
- 6 garlic cloves, smashed and cut into thirds
- 3 tablespoons vegetable oil
- ½ teaspoon ground cumin
- ½ teaspoon ground coriander
- ½ teaspoon kosher salt

For the Sauce

- 2 tablespoons tahini (sesame paste)
- 2 tablespoons hot water
- 1 tablespoon fresh lemon juice
- 1 teaspoon minced garlic
- ½ teaspoon kosher salt

1. **For the cauliflower:** In a large bowl, combine the cauliflower florets and garlic. Drizzle with the vegetable oil. Sprinkle with the cumin, coriander, and salt. Toss until well coated.

2. Place the cauliflower in the air-fryer basket. Set the air fryer to 400°F for 20 minutes, turning the cauliflower halfway through the cooking time.

3. **Meanwhile, for the sauce:** In a small bowl, combine the tahini, water, lemon juice, garlic, and salt. (The sauce will appear curdled at first, but keep stirring until you have a thick, creamy, smooth mixture.)

4. Transfer the cauliflower to a large serving bowl. Pour the sauce over and toss gently to coat. Serve immediately.

SHAWARMA GREEN BEANS

PREP TIME: 5 MINUTES

COOK TIME: 10 MINUTES

TOTAL TIME: 15 MINUTES

COOK TEMPERATURE: 375°F

DIETARY CONSIDERATIONS:
GRAIN-FREE, GLUTEN-FREE,
EGG-FREE, NUT-FREE,
SOY-FREE, DAIRY-FREE,
VEGAN, VEGETARIAN,
LOW-CARB

I created a shawarma spice mix (page 183) that's been very popular. Although I typically use that for meats, I tried it with green beans one day and decided green bean shawarma had to be a thing. So yes, I do realize that this isn't a traditional dish—but make it, and tell me if you care, because it's easy, kid-friendly, and delicious.   **SERVINGS: 2**

2 cups halved fresh green beans

2 tablespoons vegetable oil

1 tablespoon Lebanese Shawarma Spice Mix (page 183)

½ teaspoon kosher salt

1. In a medium bowl, toss together the green beans, vegetable oil, spice mix, and salt until well coated.

2. Place the seasoned green beans in the air-fryer basket. Set the air fryer to 375°F for 10 minutes, shaking the basket halfway through the cooking time.

VEGETABLES

INDIAN EGGPLANT BHARTA

The traditional way to char eggplant for bharta is over a gas stove. That's a messy, delicate proposition, and I've burned myself a time or two trying it. Plus, the mess of that charred skin flying all over the stove? I can't deal with it. I made a recipe for this in my Instant Pot that's very good—but can I be honest? It's not as good as this one. You really need a good char on the eggplant, and the air fryer does it easily and neatly.   **SERVINGS: 4**

PREP TIME: 10 MINUTES

COOK TIME: 20 MINUTES

STANDING TIME: 15 MINUTES

TOTAL TIME: 45 MINUTES

COOK TEMPERATURE: 400°F

DIETARY CONSIDERATIONS: GRAIN-FREE, GLUTEN-FREE, EGG-FREE, NUT-FREE, SOY-FREE, DAIRY-FREE, VEGAN, VEGETARIAN, LOW-CARB

1   medium eggplant

2   tablespoons vegetable oil

½   cup finely minced onion

½   cup finely chopped fresh tomato

2   tablespoons fresh lemon juice

2   tablespoons chopped fresh cilantro

½   teaspoon kosher salt

⅛   teaspoon cayenne pepper

1. Rub the eggplant all over with the vegetable oil. Place the eggplant in the air-fryer basket. Set the air fryer to 400°F for 20 minutes, or until the eggplant skin is blistered and charred.

2. Transfer the eggplant to a resealable plastic bag, seal, and set aside for 15 to 20 minutes (the eggplant will finish cooking in the residual heat trapped in the bag).

3. Transfer the eggplant to a large bowl. Peel off and discard the charred skin. Roughly mash the eggplant flesh. Add the onion, tomato, lemon juice, cilantro, salt, and cayenne. Stir to combine.

LEBANESE BABA GHANOUSH

This smoky eggplant dip is so super simple to make, you may find yourself adding eggplant to your weekly shopping list. You can serve this with pita chips, but why not go all out and make the Chicken Shawarma (page 63) and Tzatziki (page 188), add this dip, and have yourself a feast that's better than any take-out?   **SERVINGS: 4**

PREP TIME: 10 MINUTES

COOK TIME: 20 MINUTES

STANDING TIME: 15 MINUTES

TOTAL TIME: 45 MINUTES

COOK TEMPERATURE: 400°F

DIETARY CONSIDERATIONS:
GRAIN-FREE, GLUTEN-FREE,
EGG-FREE, NUT-FREE,
SOY-FREE, DAIRY-FREE,
VEGAN, VEGETARIAN,
LOW-CARB

1 medium eggplant

2 tablespoons vegetable oil

2 tablespoons tahini (sesame paste)

2 tablespoons fresh lemon juice

½ teaspoon kosher salt

1 tablespoon extra-virgin olive oil

½ teaspoon smoked paprika

2 tablespoons chopped fresh parsley

1. Rub the eggplant all over with the vegetable oil. Place the eggplant in the air-fryer basket. Set the air fryer to 400°F for 20 minutes, or until the eggplant skin is blistered and charred.

2. Transfer the eggplant to a resealable plastic bag, seal, and set aside for 15 minutes (the eggplant will finish cooking in the residual heat trapped in the bag).

3. Transfer the eggplant to a large bowl. Peel off and discard the charred skin. Roughly mash the eggplant flesh. Add the tahini, lemon juice, and salt. Stir to combine.

4. Transfer the mixture to a serving bowl. Drizzle with the olive oil. Sprinkle with the paprika and parsley and serve.

SOUTHWESTERN ROASTED CORN

I wasn't sure this would work at all, since I had corn kernels in an air-fryer basket, but not only did it work well, it was actually crazy delicious. If your basket has larger holes or a wire grid, you may need to use a smaller pan inside the air fryer. I can see how this, along with a little yogurt-based salad, would make a wonderful light supper. Or you could serve it as a side dish with grilled meats.

SERVINGS: 4

PREP TIME: 10 MINUTES

COOK TIME: 10 MINUTES

TOTAL TIME: 20 MINUTES

COOK TEMPERATURE: 375°F

DIETARY CONSIDERATIONS: GRAIN-FREE, GLUTEN-FREE, EGG-FREE, NUT-FREE, SOY-FREE, VEGETARIAN

For the Corn

- 1½ cups thawed frozen corn kernels
- 1 cup diced yellow onion
- 1 cup mixed diced bell peppers
- 1 jalapeño, diced
- 1 tablespoon fresh lemon juice
- 1 teaspoon ground cumin
- ½ teaspoon ancho chile powder
- ½ teaspoon kosher salt

For Serving

- ¼ cup queso fresco or feta cheese
- ¼ cup chopped fresh cilantro
- 1 tablespoon fresh lemon juice

1. **For the corn:** In a large bowl, stir together the corn, onion, bell peppers, jalapeño, lemon juice, cumin, chile powder, and salt until well incorporated.

2. Pour the spiced vegetables into the air-fryer basket. Set the air fryer to 375°F for 10 minutes, stirring halfway through the cooking time.

3. Transfer the corn mixture to a serving bowl. Add the cheese, cilantro, and lemon juice and stir well to combine. Serve immediately.

POTATO FRIES

Confession time: Once or twice, I have been known to overthink certain things (shocker!). This recipe is a case in point. I made these five different ways (parboiling, slicing this way or that, using three different types of potatoes, etc.). Really this was the best way. Ask for Netted Gem or baking potatoes at the grocery store, and cut them exactly as I instruct, and you, too, can have delicious fries in 30 minutes, with no additives or weird ingredients.   SERVINGS: 2

PREP TIME: 10 MINUTES

COOK TIME: 20 MINUTES

TOTAL TIME: 30 MINUTES

COOK TEMPERATURE: 400°F

DIETARY CONSIDERATIONS: GRAIN-FREE*, GLUTEN-FREE*, EGG-FREE*, NUT-FREE, SOY-FREE*, DAIRY-FREE, VEGAN*, VEGETARIAN

1   large baking potato, peeled

2   tablespoons vegetable oil

½   teaspoon kosher salt

1   teaspoon black pepper

Gochujang Mayonnaise (page 120), for dipping

1. Cut the potato lengthwise into ¼-inch-thick slices. Lay each slice flat and cut lengthwise into fries about ¼ inch thick

2. In a medium bowl, toss together the potatoes, vegetable oil, salt, and pepper until well coated.

3. Place the fries in a single layer in the air-fryer basket. (If they won't fit in a single layer, set a rack or trivet on top of the bottom layer of potatoes and place the rest of the potatoes on the rack.) Set the air fryer to 400°F for 20 minutes, shaking halfway through the cooking time, until the fries are crisp and lightly browned.

4. Turn the fries out onto a serving platter. Serve immediately with gochujang mayonnaise for dipping.

NOTE:

★ If you eat vegan or are egg-free, gluten-free, soy-free, or grain-free, use a different dipping sauce.

ROOT VEGGIE SHOESTRING FRIES WITH SAFFRON MAYONNAISE

PREP TIME: 20 MINUTES

COOK TIME: 15 MINUTES

TOTAL TIME: 35 MINUTES

COOK TEMPERATURE: 400°F

DIETARY CONSIDERATIONS: GRAIN-FREE, GLUTEN-FREE, NUT-FREE, SOY-FREE, DAIRY-FREE, PALEO*

These colorful fries are so beautiful and so easy to make, you'll find yourself making them for company, as well as to add a little cheer to everyday meals. Make the recipe as written once, and then try varying the spices to create your own recipe.   **SERVINGS: 4**

For the Fries

- 1   large beet, peeled,
- 2   medium sweet potatoes, peeled
- 2   tablespoons extra-virgin olive oil
- ½   teaspoon garlic powder
- ½   teaspoon smoked paprika
- ½   teaspoon kosher salt
- ¼   teaspoon black pepper

For the Mayonnaise

- 1   tablespoon chicken broth, warmed
- ¼   teaspoon saffron threads
- ½   cup mayonnaise
- ⅛   teaspoon cayenne pepper
- 1   tablespoon fresh lemon juice

1. **For the fries:** Cut the beet and sweet potato into pieces that fit your spiralizer (use the blade that will produce the thickest strands). Spiralize the beet and sweet potato. Cut the strands into 4-inch sections. (Alternatively, use a mandoline to julienne.)

2. Place the spiralized beet between two double-thick layers of paper towels. Squeeze out as much liquid as possible. Place the beet in a large bowl. Repeat with the sweet potatoes, using clean paper towels, and place in a separate large bowl.

3. Drizzle the beet with 1 tablespoon of the olive oil. Sprinkle with half the garlic powder, paprika, salt, and pepper. Toss until everything is evenly coated. Repeat with the sweet potato.

4. Transfer the beet to the air-fryer basket. Set the air fryer to 400°F for 15 minutes, gently tossing the beet with tongs every 5 minutes, until crisp and lightly browned. Repeat with the sweet potatoes.

5. **Meanwhile, for the mayonnaise:** In a small bowl, stir together the broth and saffron. Let steep for 5 minutes. Add the mayonnaise, cayenne, and lemon juice. Stir until well blended.

6. Serve the beet and sweet potato fries immediately, with the saffron mayonnaise for dipping.

NOTE:

★   If you eat Paleo, use a compliant avocado oil-based mayonnaise.

ASIAN TOFU SALAD

I try to give you recipes that you can make once as written, then play around with. This is one of those recipes. Once you see how easy it is to air-fry tofu, you can use different sauces and, of course, different vegetables. I think this tofu would go brilliantly with the peanut sauce on page 185 if you need a quick appetizer. Use extra-firm tofu and don't worry about pressing it to drain excess liquid. Just slap it in the marinade, air-fry it, and you're good to go. **SERVINGS: 2**

PREP TIME: 15 MINUTES

STANDING TIME: 10 MINUTES

COOK TIME: 15 MINUTES

TOTAL TIME: 40 MINUTES

COOK TEMPERATURE: 400°F

DIETARY CONSIDERATIONS: EGG-FREE, NUT-FREE, DAIRY-FREE, VEGAN, VEGETARIAN, LOW-CARB

For the Tofu

- 1 tablespoon soy sauce
- 1 tablespoon vegetable oil
- 1 teaspoon minced fresh ginger
- 1 teaspoon minced garlic
- 8 ounces extra-firm tofu, drained and cubed

For the Salad

- ¼ cup rice vinegar
- 1 tablespoon sugar
- 1 teaspoon salt
- 1 teaspoon black pepper
- ¼ cup sliced scallions
- 1 cup julienned cucumber
- 1 cup julienned red onion
- 1 cup julienned carrots
- 6 butter lettuce leaves

1. **For the tofu:** In a small bowl, whisk together the soy sauce, vegetable oil, ginger, and garlic. Add the tofu and mix gently. Let stand at room temperature for 10 minutes.

2. Arrange the tofu in a single layer in the air-fryer basket. Set the air fryer to 400°F for 15 minutes, shaking halfway through the cooking time.

3. **Meanwhile, for the salad:** In a large bowl, whisk together the vinegar, sugar, salt, pepper, and scallions. Add the cucumber, onion, and carrots and toss to combine. Set aside to marinate while the tofu cooks.

4. To serve, arrange three lettuce leaves on each of two plates. Pile the marinated vegetables (and marinade) on the lettuce. Divide the tofu between the plates and serve.

POTATOES ANNA

This is a perfect, perfect thing to make in your air fryer. You do need to place the pan over the stovetop to properly brown the bottom. Other than that, though, it's basically potatoes, butter, salt, and pepper—doesn't that just sound delicious? Don't skimp on the butter! Use my directions as a guideline and use as much or as little of the butter and seasonings as you need to coat and season the potatoes well. One note: Don't rinse the sliced potatoes or soak them in water—you need all their starch to get the layers to bind together.

SERVINGS: 4

PREP TIME: 15 MINUTES

COOK TIME: 40 MINUTES

TOTAL TIME: 55 MINUTES

COOK TEMPERATURE: 400°F

DIETARY CONSIDERATIONS: GRAIN-FREE, GLUTEN-FREE, EGG-FREE, NUT-FREE, SOY-FREE, VEGETARIAN

4 tablespoons (½ stick) salted butter, melted

1 large potato, peeled and cut into ⅛-inch-thick slices on a mandoline

1 teaspoon kosher salt

1 teaspoon black pepper

1. Brush the bottom of a flameproof 7 inch round baking pan with some of the butter. Place one slice of potato in the middle of the pan. Create concentric, overlapping circles of potato around the first potato slice, making sure you go all the way to the edges of the pan (the potatoes will shrink as they cook). Brush the first layer with butter and season lightly with some of the salt and pepper.

2. Place the pan on the stovetop over medium heat. Cook until the bottom layer is nicely browned. Remove the pan from the stove and continue layering the potatoes in concentric circles, generously brushing each layer with butter and seasoning between the layers. Press down on the layers as you work. Pour any remaining butter over the potatoes. Season with any remaining salt and pepper.

3. Cover the pan tightly with aluminum foil. Place the pan in the air-fryer basket. Set the air fryer to 400°F for 30 minutes. Remove the foil and cook for 10 minutes more.

4. To serve, use a thin metal spatula or butter knife to loosen the edges of the potatoes. Place a serving plate over the pan. Invert the pan and the plate together to unmold the potatoes onto the plate and serve hot.

WARM SALADE NIÇOISE

PREP TIME: 15 MINUTES

COOK TIME: 15 MINUTES

TOTAL TIME: 30 MINUTES

COOK TEMPERATURE: 400°F

DIETARY CONSIDERATIONS:
GRAIN-FREE, GLUTEN-FREE,
NUT-FREE, SOY-FREE,
DAIRY-FREE

Traditional salade Niçoise features steamed or boiled potatoes, green beans, and, often, canned tuna. This air-fryer version uses fresh tuna and gives both the tuna and potatoes a nice crispy crust. It's also a very handy way to make an entire meal with fish, potatoes, and vegetables all at the same time.   **SERVINGS: 2**

For the Salad

- 6 new potatoes, quartered
- 1 cup halved slender green beans
- 1 cup grape tomatoes
- 2 teaspoons vegetable oil, plus more as needed

  Kosher salt and black pepper

- 2 (4-ounce) tuna fillets (about 1 inch thick), cut in half

For the Vinaigrette

- 2 tablespoons extra-virgin olive oil
- 1 tablespoon red or white wine vinegar
- 1 teaspoon Dijon mustard
- ¼ teaspoon herbes de Provence (optional)
- ⅛ teaspoon kosher salt

  Black pepper

For Serving

- 6 butter lettuce leaves
- 2 hard-cooked large eggs (page 6), peeled and halved
- 10 Niçoise olives

1. **For the salad:** In a small bowl, toss the potatoes, green beans, and grape tomatoes with the vegetable oil. Season with salt and pepper. Arrange the vegetables in a single layer in the air-fryer basket. Set the air fryer to 400°F for 10 minutes, shaking halfway through the cooking time.

2. Brush the tuna on both sides with vegetable oil and season to taste with salt and pepper. Press the salt and pepper into the tuna so they will stay put. After the vegetables have cooked for 10 minutes, add the tuna to the basket on top of the vegetables. Cook for 5 minutes for medium-well tuna.

3. Transfer the tuna to a cutting board and let it rest for 5 minutes. Slice the tuna thinly across the grain.

4. **Meanwhile, for the vinaigrette:** In a small jar with a lid, combine the olive oil, vinegar, mustard, herbes de Provence (if using), salt, and pepper to taste. Shake to combine.

5. Place three lettuce leaves on each of two dinner plates. Arrange the tuna and vegetables on the lettuce. Place two egg halves on each plate. Scatter the olives over. Drizzle with the vinaigrette. Serve immediately.

CHICKEN

AFRICAN PIRI-PIRI CHICKEN DRUMSTICKS

PREP TIME: 15 MINUTES

MARINATING TIME:
30 MINUTES

COOK TIME: 20 MINUTES

TOTAL TIME: 65 MINUTES

COOK TEMPERATURE: 400°F

DIETARY CONSIDERATIONS:
GRAIN-FREE, GLUTEN-FREE,
EGG-FREE, NUT-FREE,
SOY-FREE, DAIRY-FREE,
PALEO*, LOW-CARB

This slightly spicy chicken dish originated in Africa, after the Portuguese brought chile peppers into Mozambique. (Piri-piri means "chile" in Swahili.) Luckily for you, you don't have to go to Mozambique or Portugal to enjoy all the great spicy goodness of this piri-piri chicken. Bottled piri-piri sauce is available at specialty markets and online. You can substitute another hot sauce, like Tabasco. **SERVINGS: 2**

For the Chicken

- 1 tablespoon chopped fresh thyme leaves
- 1 tablespoon minced fresh ginger
- 1 small shallot, finely chopped
- 2 garlic cloves, minced
- 1/3 cup piri-piri sauce or hot sauce
- 3 tablespoons extra-virgin olive oil
- Zest and juice of 1 lemon
- 1 teaspoon smoked paprika
- 1/2 teaspoon kosher salt
- 1/2 teaspoon black pepper
- 4 chicken drumsticks

For the Glaze

- 2 tablespoons butter or ghee (page 187)
- 1 teaspoon chopped fresh thyme leaves
- 1 garlic clove, minced
- 1 tablespoon piri-piri sauce
- 1 tablespoon fresh lemon juice

1. **For the chicken:** In a small bowl, stir together all the ingredients except the chicken. Place the chicken and the marinade in a gallon-size resealable plastic bag. Seal the bag and massage to coat. Refrigerate for at least 2 hours or up to 24 hours, turning the bag occasionally.

2. Place the chicken legs in the air-fryer basket. Set the air fryer to 400°F for 20 minutes, turning the chicken halfway through the cooking time.

3. **Meanwhile, for the glaze:** Melt the butter in a small saucepan over medium-high heat. Add the thyme and garlic. Cook, stirring, until the garlic just begins to brown, 1 to 2 minutes. Add the piri-piri sauce and lemon juice. Reduce the heat to medium-low and simmer for 1 to 2 minutes.

4. Transfer the chicken to a serving platter. Pour the glaze over the chicken. Serve immediately.

NOTE:

★ If you eat Paleo, use a compliant piri-piri sauce, and ghee instead of butter.

AFRICAN MERGUEZ MEATBALLS

Merguez sausages are typically made with lamb, but not everyone has easy access to lamb, so I decided to make these with chicken instead. Of course, once you try this recipe and decide you love it (as I'm sure you will), you can experiment with different types of ground meat and see which you like best.   **SERVINGS: 4**

PREP TIME: 10 MINUTES

COOK TIME: 10 MINUTES

STANDING TIME: 30 MINUTES

TOTAL TIME: 50 MINUTES

COOK TEMPERATURE: 400°F

DIETARY CONSIDERATIONS:
GRAIN-FREE, GLUTEN-FREE,
EGG-FREE, NUT-FREE,
SOY-FREE, DAIRY-FREE,
LOW-CARB

- 1 **pound ground chicken**
- 2 **garlic cloves, finely minced**
- 1 **tablespoon sweet Hungarian paprika**
- 1 **teaspoon kosher salt**
- 1 **teaspoon sugar**
- 1 **teaspoon ground cumin**
- ½ **teaspoon black pepper**
- ½ **teaspoon ground fennel**
- ½ **teaspoon ground coriander**
- ½ **teaspoon cayenne pepper**
- ¼ **teaspoon ground allspice**

1. In a large bowl, gently mix the chicken, garlic, paprika, salt, sugar, cumin, black pepper, fennel, coriander, cayenne, and allspice until all the ingredients are incorporated. Let stand for 30 minutes at room temperature, or cover and refrigerate for up to 24 hours.

2. Form the mixture into 16 meatballs. Arrange them in a single layer in the air-fryer basket. Set the air fryer to 400°F for 10 minutes, turning the meatballs halfway through the cooking time. Use a meat thermometer to ensure the meatballs have reached an internal temperature of 165°F.

CHICKEN & VEGETABLE FAJITAS

This recipe appeals to the lazy/efficient side of me. Making meat and vegetables in one shot? Yes, please. Once again, use this as a base recipe and mix up the flavors. You could use a store-bought chicken rub, berbere spice mix, or shawarma mix (page 63) and enjoy various types of "fajitas." Serve with tortillas, guacamole, salsa, and sour cream for a bit of variety.

SERVINGS: 6

PREP TIME: 15 MINUTES

COOK TIME: 23 MINUTES

TOTAL TIME: 40 MINUTES

COOK TEMPERATURE: 375°F

DIETARY CONSIDERATIONS: GRAIN-FREE*, GLUTEN-FREE*, EGG-FREE, NUT-FREE, LOW-CARB*, SOY-FREE

For the Chicken

- 1 pound boneless, skinless chicken thighs, cut crosswise into thirds
- 1 tablespoon vegetable oil
- 4½ teaspoons taco seasoning

For the Vegetables

- 1 cup sliced onion
- 1 cup sliced bell pepper
- 1 or 2 jalapeños, quartered lengthwise
- 1 tablespoon vegetable oil
- ½ teaspoon kosher salt
- ½ teaspoon ground cumin

For Serving

Tortillas

Sour cream

Shredded cheese

Guacamole

Salsa

1. **For the chicken:** In a medium bowl, toss together the chicken, vegetable oil, and taco seasoning to coat.

2. **For the vegetables:** In a separate bowl, toss together the onion, bell pepper, jalapeño(s), vegetable oil, salt, and cumin to coat.

3. Place the chicken in the air-fryer basket. Set the air fryer to 375°F for 10 minutes. Add the vegetables to the basket, toss everything together to blend the seasonings, and set the air fryer for 13 minutes more. Use a meat thermometer to ensure the chicken has reached an internal temperature of 165°F.

4. Transfer the chicken and vegetables to a serving platter. Serve with tortillas and the desired fajita fixings.

NOTE:

★ To make this low-carb, gluten-free, and grain-free, omit tortillas and wrap in lettuce leaves instead.

CHICKEN SHAWARMA

Give me a good chicken shawarma with some tzatziki—and don't talk to me until I'm done eating them, because I really need to focus on how good they taste together! Take my advice—make the shawarma spice yourself; nothing compares to freshly ground spices.   **SERVINGS: 4**

PREP TIME: 10 MINUTES

MARINATING TIME: 30 MINUTES

COOK TIME: 15 MINUTES

TOTAL TIME: 55 MINUTES

COOK TEMPERATURE: 350°F

DIETARY CONSIDERATIONS: EGG-FREE, NUT-FREE, SOY-FREE

For the Shawarma Spice

- 2 teaspoons dried oregano
- 1 teaspoon ground cinnamon
- 1 teaspoon ground cumin
- 1 teaspoon ground coriander
- 1 teaspoon kosher salt
- ½ teaspoon ground allspice
- ½ teaspoon cayenne pepper

For the Chicken

- 1 pound boneless, skinless chicken thighs, cut into large bite-size chunks
- 2 tablespoons vegetable oil

For Serving

- Tzatziki (page 188)
- Pita bread

1. **For the shawarma spice:** In a small bowl, combine the oregano, cayenne, cumin, coriander, salt, cinnamon, and allspice.

2. For the chicken: In a large bowl, toss together the chicken, vegetable oil, and shawarma spice to coat. Marinate at room temperature for 30 minutes or cover and refrigerate for up to 24 hours.

3. Place the chicken in the air-fryer basket. Set the air fryer to 350°F for 15 minutes, or until the chicken reaches an internal temperature of 165°F.

4. Transfer the chicken to a serving platter. Serve with tzatziki and pita bread.

COCONUT CHICKEN MEATBALLS

This recipe came about when I was searching for a way to make low-carb meatballs without a bread crumb binder. The good thing about using coconut is that you add both taste and a little bit of body to the meatballs in one fell swoop. Some sweet chili sauce would go very well with these meatballs. **SERVINGS: 4**

PREP TIME: 10 MINUTES

COOK TIME: 14 MINUTES

TOTAL TIME: 24 MINUTES

COOK TEMPERATURE: 350°F/400°F

DIETARY CONSIDERATIONS: EGG-FREE, NUT-FREE, DAIRY-FREE

1 pound ground chicken

2 scallions, finely chopped

1 cup chopped fresh cilantro leaves

¼ cup unsweetened shredded coconut

1 tablespoon hoisin sauce

1 tablespoon soy sauce

2 teaspoons sriracha or other hot sauce

1 teaspoon toasted sesame oil

½ teaspoon kosher salt

1 teaspoon black pepper

1. In a large bowl, gently mix the chicken, scallions, cilantro, coconut, hoisin, soy sauce, sriracha, sesame oil, salt, and pepper until thoroughly combined (the mixture will be wet and sticky).

2. Place a sheet of parchment paper in the air-fryer basket. Using a small scoop or teaspoon, drop rounds of the mixture in a single layer onto the parchment paper.

3. Set the air fryer to 350°F for 10 minutes, turning the meatballs halfway through the cooking time. Raise the air-fryer temperature to 400°F and cook for 4 minutes more to brown the outsides of the meatballs. Use a meat thermometer to ensure the meatballs have reached an internal temperature of 165°F.

4. Transfer the meatballs to a serving platter. Repeat with any remaining chicken mixture.

THAI-STYLE CORNISH GAME HENS (GAI YANG)

Making these Cornish hens is a sensual experience. As you start to grind the ingredients for the marinade together, you will know instantly how good this dish is going to taste. Your sense of smell works overtime, making your mouth water—and that's even before you smell the birds cooking! This recipe is a must-make. If you can't find prepared lemongrass paste, coarsely chop some fresh lemongrass stalks and add them to the mixture in its place.

SERVINGS: 4

PREP TIME: 15 MINUTES

MARINATING TIME: 30 MINUTES

COOK TIME: 20 MINUTES

TOTAL TIME: 1 HOUR 5 MINUTES

COOK TEMPERATURE: 400°F

DIETARY CONSIDERATIONS: EGG-FREE, NUT-FREE, DAIRY-FREE

- 1 cup chopped fresh cilantro leaves and stems
- ¼ cup fish sauce
- 1 tablespoon soy sauce
- 1 serrano chile, seeded and chopped
- 8 garlic cloves, smashed
- 2 tablespoons sugar
- 2 tablespoons lemongrass paste (see headnote)
- 2 teaspoons black pepper
- 2 teaspoons ground coriander
- 1 teaspoon kosher salt
- 1 teaspoon ground turmeric
- 2 Cornish game hens, giblets removed, split in half lengthwise

1. In a blender, combine the cilantro, fish sauce, soy sauce, serrano, garlic, sugar, lemongrass, black pepper, coriander, salt, and turmeric. Blend until smooth.

2. Place the game hen halves in a large bowl. Pour the cilantro mixture over the hen halves and toss to coat. Marinate at room temperature for 30 minutes, or cover and refrigerate for up to 24 hours.

3. Arrange the hen halves in a single layer in the air-fryer basket. Set the air fryer to 400°F for 20 minutes. Use a meat thermometer to ensure the game hens have reached an internal temperature of 165°F.

CRISPY CRACKED-PEPPER CHICKEN WINGS

If I created an air-fryer cookbook without at least one breaded recipe, you'd never forgive me. So, I give you breaded chicken wings. Let's be honest with each other—breading cooked in an air fryer does not taste like breading cooked in a deep fryer. But these taste like good chicken wings, so I've included this recipe. If you plan to sauce them, cook them fully, remove from the air fryer, and toss with the sauce, then air-fry for another minute or two before serving.   **SERVINGS: 4**

PREP TIME: 15 MINUTES

COOK TIME: 20 MINUTES

TOTAL TIME: 35 MINUTES

COOK TEMPERATURE: 400°F

DIETARY CONSIDERATIONS: EGG-FREE, NUT-FREE, SOY-FREE, DAIRY-FREE

1   pound chicken wings

3   tablespoons vegetable oil

½   cup all-purpose flour

½   teaspoon smoked paprika

½   teaspoon garlic powder

½   teaspoon kosher salt

1½   teaspoons freshly cracked black pepper

1. Place the chicken wings in a large bowl. Drizzle the vegetable oil over wings and toss to coat.

2. In a separate bowl, whisk together the flour, paprika, garlic powder, salt, and pepper until combined.

3. Dredge the wings in the flour mixture one at a time, coating them well, and place in the air-fryer basket. Set the air fryer to 400°F for 20 minutes, turning the wings halfway through the cooking time, until the breading is browned and crunchy.

GOCHUJANG CHICKEN WINGS

These wings are the reason so many people in the Two Sleevers Facebook group ran out to buy air fryers. Crispy, salty, sweet, and spicy with Korean chile paste—little bites of heaven! And, of course, super easy to make. If I were you, I'd inaugurate my air fryer with this super-simple recipe.   **SERVINGS: 4**

PREP TIME: 15 MINUTES

COOK TIME: 25 MINUTES

TOTAL TIME: 40 MINUTES

COOK TEMPERATURE: 400°F

DIETARY CONSIDERATIONS: NUT-FREE, DAIRY-FREE

For the Wings

- 2 pounds chicken wings
- 1 teaspoon kosher salt
- 1 teaspoon black pepper or gochugaru (Korean red pepper)

For the Sauce

- 2 tablespoons gochujang (Korean chile paste)
- 1 tablespoon mayonnaise
- 1 tablespoon toasted sesame oil
- 1 tablespoon minced fresh ginger
- 1 tablespoon minced garlic
- 1 teaspoon sugar
- 1 teaspoon agave nectar or honey

For Serving

- 1 teaspoon sesame seeds
- ¼ cup chopped scallions

1. **For the wings:** Season the wings with the salt and pepper and place in the air-fryer basket. Set the air fryer to 400°F for 20 minutes, turning the wings halfway through the cooking time.

2. **Meanwhile, for the sauce:** In a small bowl, combine the gochujang, mayonnaise, sesame oil, ginger, garlic, sugar, and agave; set aside.

3. As you near the 20-minute mark, use a meat thermometer to check the meat. When the wings reach 160°F, transfer them to a large bowl. Pour about half the sauce on the wings; toss to coat (serve the remaining sauce as a dip).

4. Return the wings to the air-fryer basket and cook for 5 minutes, until the sauce has glazed.

5. Transfer the wings to a serving platter. Sprinkle with the sesame seeds and scallions. Serve with the reserved sauce on the side for dipping.

HAWAIIAN HULI HULI CHICKEN

We took our sons to Hawaii when they were younger. One day, everyone was starving and cranky and we happened to pass a roadside sign for huli huli chicken. The aromas of the chicken we bought drove everyone nuts, so my husband pulled over and we decided to have a roadside picnic. I swear I heard all three of them grunt like animals as they tore into that delicious chicken. This was my attempt to reproduce it, and I'm told I hit the mark. I've since banned grunting at the table, though.   **SERVINGS: 4**

PREP TIME: 10 MINUTES

MARINATING TIME: 30 MINUTES

COOK TIME: 15 MINUTES

TOTAL TIME: 55 MINUTES

COOK TEMPERATURE: 350°F

DIETARY CONSIDERATIONS: EGG-FREE, NUT-FREE, DAIRY-FREE

- 4 boneless, skinless chicken thighs (about 1½ pounds)
- 1 (8-ounce) can pineapple chunks in juice, drained, ¼ cup juice reserved
- ¼ cup soy sauce
- ¼ cup sugar
- 2 tablespoons ketchup
- 1 tablespoon minced fresh ginger
- 1 tablespoon minced garlic
- ¼ cup chopped scallions

1. Use a fork to pierce the chicken all over to allow the marinade to penetrate better. Place the chicken in a large bowl or large resealable plastic bag.

2. Set the drained pineapple chunks aside. In a small microwave-safe bowl, combine the pineapple juice, soy sauce, sugar, ketchup, ginger, and garlic. Pour half the sauce over the chicken; toss to coat. Reserve the remaining sauce. Marinate the chicken at room temperature for 30 minutes, or cover and refrigerate for up to 24 hours.

3. Place the chicken in the air-fryer basket. (Discard marinade.) Set the air fryer to 350°F for 15 minutes, turning halfway through the cooking time.

4. Meanwhile, microwave the reserved sauce on high for 45 to 60 seconds, stirring every 15 seconds, until the sauce has the consistency of a thick glaze.

5. At the end of the cooking time, use a meat thermometer to ensure the chicken has reached an internal temperature of 165°F.

6. Transfer the chicken to a serving platter. Pour the sauce over the chicken. Garnish with the pineapple chunks and scallions.

PERSIAN CHICKEN KEBABS (JOOJEH KABAB)

If you've never had joojeh kabab, you are missing out. This is very lightly spiced compared to my other recipes, but the saffron lends a wonderful, rich flavor that is incomparable. I will say that air-fried kebabs don't have the same charcoal taste of grilled joojeh, but when there's snow on the ground and you want joojeh, you won't care. Serve with grilled tomatoes and rice for a traditional meal. **SERVINGS: 4**

PREP TIME: 10 MINUTES

MARINATING TIME: 30 MINUTES

COOK TIME: 12 MINUTES

TOTAL TIME: 52 MINUTES

COOK TEMPERATURE: 350°F/400°F

DIETARY CONSIDERATIONS: GRAIN-FREE, GLUTEN-FREE, EGG-FREE, NUT-FREE, SOY-FREE, LOW-CARB

- 1 pound boneless, skinless chicken breast, cut into large, bite-size pieces
- ¼ cup sliced yellow onion
- ¼ cup plain Greek yogurt
- 1 tablespoon vegetable oil
- 1 teaspoon kosher salt
- ½ teaspoon black pepper
- tk teaspoon turmeric
- 2 tablespoons Saffron Water (recipe follows)

  Vegetable oil spray

1. In a large bowl, toss together the chicken, onion, yogurt, vegetable oil, salt, pepper, turmeric, and saffron water to coat. Marinate at room temperature for 30 minutes, or cover and refrigerate for up to 24 hours.

2. Place the chicken in a single layer in the air-fryer basket. (Discard remaining marinade.) Set the air fryer to 350°F for 10 minutes, turning the chicken and spraying it with a little vegetable oil spray halfway through the cooking time. Increase the air-fryer temperature to 400°F for 2 minutes to allow the chicken to crisp and brown a little.

SAFFRON WATER

Using a mortar and pestle, grind together ½ teaspoon saffron threads and ¼ teaspoon sugar. Mix with 1 cup water and transfer to a bottle. Store in the refrigerator until ready to use, up to a week. (If you want to skip this step, just throw a few strands of saffron into the chicken marinade and call it a day.)

SPICY INDIAN FENNEL CHICKEN

Fennel seed is quite widely used in South Indian cooking. Using ground fennel in the spice mixture lends the chicken a distinctive and unique taste. Air fryers tend to roast spices and make them very potent, so use the quantity the recipe calls for the first time, then you can adjust up or down as you prefer. Serve with naan or chapati breads, along with a light salad. You can also pair this with creamy coleslaw. **SERVINGS: 4**

PREP TIME: 10 MINUTES

MARINATING TIME: 30 MINUTES

COOK TIME: 15 MINUTES

TOTAL TIME: 55 MINUTES

COOK TEMPERATURE: 350°F

DIETARY CONSIDERATIONS: GRAIN-FREE, GLUTEN-FREE, EGG-FREE, NUT-FREE, SOY-FREE, DAIRY-FREE, LOW-CARB

- 1 pound boneless, skinless chicken thighs, cut crosswise into thirds
- 1 yellow onion, cut into 1½-inch-thick slices
- 1 tablespoon coconut oil, melted
- 2 teaspoons minced fresh ginger
- 2 teaspoons minced garlic
- 1 teaspoon smoked paprika
- 1 teaspoon ground fennel
- 1 teaspoon Garam Masala (page 181)
- 1 teaspoon ground turmeric
- 1 teaspoon kosher salt
- ½ to 1 teaspoon cayenne pepper
- Vegetable oil spray
- 2 teaspoons fresh lemon juice
- ¼ cup chopped fresh cilantro or parsley

1. Use a fork to pierce the chicken all over to allow the marinade to penetrate better.

2. In a large bowl, combine the onion, coconut oil, ginger, garlic, paprika, fennel, garam masala, turmeric, salt, and cayenne. Add the chicken, toss to combine, and marinate at room temperature for 30 minutes, or cover and refrigerate for up to 24 hours.

3. Place the chicken and onion in the air-fryer basket. (Discard remaining marinade.) Spray with some vegetable oil spray. Set the air fryer to 350°F for 15 minutes. Halfway through the cooking time, remove the basket, spray the chicken and onion with more vegetable oil spray, and toss gently to coat. At the end of the cooking time, use a meat thermometer to ensure the chicken has reached an internal temperature of 165°F.

6. Transfer the chicken and onion to a serving platter. Sprinkle with the lemon juice and cilantro and serve.

TANDOORI CHICKEN

Can I brag about this recipe? It's the real deal. This tandoori isn't not red like you see in restaurants because I didn't use the fake red coloring that restaurants do. It isn't bland like the kind most American restaurants make—because tandoori chicken isn't supposed to be bland. These are good, robust, authentic little bites of tandoori chicken, just the way it's served in India. A cooling raita makes a great accompaniment. **SERVINGS: 4**

PREP TIME: 10 MINUTES

**MARINATING TIME:
30 MINUTES**

COOK TIME: 15 MINUTES

COOK TEMPERATURE: 350°F

TOTAL TIME: 55 MINUTES

**DIETARY CONSIDERATIONS:
GRAIN-FREE, GLUTEN-FREE,
EGG-FREE, NUT-FREE,
SOY-FREE, LOW-CARB**

- 1 pound chicken tenders, halved crosswise
- ¼ cup plain Greek yogurt
- 1 tablespoon minced fresh ginger
- 1 tablespoon minced garlic
- ¼ cup chopped fresh cilantro or parsley
- 1 teaspoon kosher salt
- ½ to 1 teaspoon cayenne pepper
- 1 teaspoon ground turmeric
- 1 teaspoon Garam Masala (page 181)
- 1 teaspoon sweet smoked paprika
- 1 tablespoon vegetable oil or melted ghee (page 187)
- 2 teaspoons fresh lemon juice
- 2 tablespoons chopped fresh cilantro

1. In a large glass bowl, toss together the chicken, yogurt, ginger, garlic, cilantro, salt, cayenne, turmeric, garam masala, and paprika to coat. Marinate at room temperature for 30 minutes, or cover and refrigerate for up to 24 hours.

2. Place the chicken in a single layer in the air-fryer basket. (Discard remaining marinade.) Spray the chicken with oil. Set the air fryer to 350°F for 15 minutes. Halfway through the cooking time, spray the chicken with more vegetable oil spray, and toss gently to coat. Cook for 5 minutes more.

3. Transfer the chicken to a serving platter. Sprinkle with lemon juice and toss to coat. Sprinkle with the cilantro and serve.

THAI CURRY MEATBALLS

Using a prepared curry paste makes these meatballs a snap. You can use red, green, or yellow curry paste as you prefer. The peanut sauce on page 185 makes a lovely accompaniment.

SERVINGS: 4

PREP TIME: 10 MINUTES

COOK TIME: 10 MINUTES

TOTAL TIME: 20 MINUTES

COOK TEMPERATURE: 400°F

DIETARY CONSIDERATIONS: GRAIN-FREE, GLUTEN-FREE, EGG-FREE, NUT-FREE, SOY-FREE, DAIRY-FREE, PALEO*, LOW-CARB

1 pound ground chicken

¼ cup chopped fresh cilantro

1 teaspoon chopped fresh mint

1 tablespoon fresh lime juice

1 tablespoon Thai red, green, or yellow curry paste

1 tablespoon fish sauce

2 garlic cloves, minced

2 teaspoons minced fresh ginger

½ teaspoon kosher salt

½ teaspoon black pepper

¼ teaspoon red pepper flakes

1. In a large bowl, gently mix the ground chicken, cilantro, mint, lime juice, curry paste, fish sauce, garlic, ginger, salt, black pepper, and red pepper flakes until thoroughly combined.

2. Form the mixture into 16 meatballs. Place the meatballs in a single layer in the air-fryer basket. Set the air fryer to 400°F for 10 minutes, turning the meatballs halfway through the cooking time. Use a meat thermometer to ensure the meatballs have reached an internal temperature of 165°F.

NOTE:

★ If you eat Paleo, use a brand of fish sauce that doesn't contain sugar, such as Red Boat.

TURKISH CHICKEN KEBABS (TAVUK SHISH)

I love using chicken in many different forms, with just a twist of spices. These tavuk shish are a traditional Turkish recipe that is very approachable, even for those who aren't particularly adventurous eaters. They've been a huge hit with my readers. Serve with bread or rice and a steamed vegetable.   **SERVINGS: 4**

PREP TIME: 15 MINUTES

MARINATING TIME: 30 MINUTES

COOK TIME: 15 MINUTES

TOTAL TIME: 1 HOUR

COOK TEMPERATURE: 375°F

DIETARY CONSIDERATIONS: GRAIN-FREE, GLUTEN-FREE, EGG-FREE, NUT-FREE, SOY-FREE, LOW-CARB

¼ cup plain Greek yogurt

1 tablespoon minced garlic

1 tablespoon tomato paste

1 tablespoon fresh lemon juice

1 tablespoon vegetable oil

1 teaspoon kosher salt

1 teaspoon ground cumin

1 teaspoon sweet Hungarian paprika

½ teaspoon ground cinnamon

½ teaspoon black pepper

½ teaspoon cayenne pepper

1 pound boneless, skinless chicken thighs, quartered crosswise

1. In a large bowl, combine the yogurt, garlic, tomato paste, lemon juice, vegetable oil, salt, cumin, paprika, cinnamon, black pepper, and cayenne. Stir until the spices are blended into the yogurt.

2. Add the chicken to the bowl and toss until well coated. Marinate at room temperature for 30 minutes, or cover and refrigerate for up to 24 hours.

3. Arrange the chicken in a single layer in the air-fryer basket. Set the air fryer to 375°F for 10 minutes. Turn the chicken and cook for 5 minutes more. Use a meat thermometer to ensure the chicken has reached an internal temperature of 165°F.

YELLOW CURRY BAKED CHICKEN

I tried this recipe for grins and giggles, and when it worked out, I was so delighted that I had to share it with you. Who ever heard of making a curry in an air fryer? Well, you just did. Much to my surprise, it works, and with very little effort, stirring, or monitoring. Once you master this recipe, you'll be able to think of other stews and curries you want to cook in your air fryer.

SERVINGS: 6

PREP TIME: 10 MINUTES

MARINATING TIME: 30 MINUTES

COOK TIME: 20 MINUTES

TOTAL TIME: 1 HOUR

COOK TEMPERATURE: 375°F

DIETARY CONSIDERATIONS: GRAIN-FREE, GLUTEN-FREE, EGG-FREE, SOY-FREE, DAIRY-FREE, LOW-CARB

- ½ cup unsweetened full-fat coconut milk
- 2 tablespoons yellow curry paste (see Note)
- 1 tablespoon minced fresh ginger
- 1 tablespoon minced garlic
- 1 teaspoon kosher salt
- 1 pound boneless, skinless chicken thighs, halved crosswise
- 2 tablespoons chopped peanuts

1. In a large bowl, stir together the coconut milk, curry paste, ginger, garlic, and salt until well blended. Add the chicken; toss well to coat. Marinate at room temperature for 30 minutes, or cover and refrigerate for up to 24 hours.

2. Place the chicken (along with marinade) in a 7-inch round baking pan with 4-inch sides. Place the pan in the air-fryer basket. Set the air fryer to 375°F for 20 minutes, turning the chicken halfway through the cooking time. Use a meat thermometer to ensure the chicken has reached an internal temperature of 165°F.

3. Sprinkle the chicken with the chopped peanuts and serve.

NOTE:

★ Yellow curry paste can be found in specialty markets or online; Thai green curry paste is a more widely available option and a fine substitute, though the color will be a little different.

GREEK CHICKEN SOUVLAKI

Souvlaki is a popular Greek dish that is often made by skewering seasoned meats and vegetables together. Although souvla means "skewer" in Greek, you'll forgo the skewers in this recipe. I tested kebabs and chicken on and off the skewers and found that the skewers really didn't help at all in air-frying and instead just created an unnecessary step. **SERVINGS: 3 OR 4**

PREP TIME: 20 MINUTES

MARINATING TIME: 30 MINUTES

COOK TIME: 15 MINUTES

TOTAL TIME: 1 HOUR 5 MINUTES

COOK TEMPERATURE: 350°F/400°F

DIETARY CONSIDERATIONS: EGG-FREE, NUT-FREE, SOY-FREE, GRAIN-FREE*, GLUTEN-FREE*, LOW-CARB*

For the Chicken

Grated zest and juice of 1 lemon

2 tablespoons extra-virgin olive oil

1 tablespoon Greek souvlaki seasoning

1 pound boneless, skinless chicken breast, cut into 2-inch chunks

Vegetable oil spray

For Serving

Warm pita bread or hot cooked rice

Sliced ripe tomatoes

Sliced cucumbers

Thinly sliced red onion

Kalamata olives

Tzatziki (page 188)

1. **For the chicken:** In a small bowl, combine the lemon zest, lemon juice, olive oil, and souvlaki seasoning. Place the chicken in a gallon-size resealable plastic bag. Pour the marinade over chicken. Seal bag and massage to coat. Place the bag in a large bowl and marinate for 30 minutes, or cover and refrigerate up to 24 hours, turning the bag occasionally.

2. Place the chicken a single layer in the air-fryer basket. Set the air fryer to 350°F for 10 minutes, turning the chicken and spraying with a little vegetable oil spray halfway through the cooking time. Increase the air-fryer temperature to 400°F for 5 minutes to allow the chicken to crisp and brown a little.

3. Transfer the chicken to a serving platter and serve with pita bread or rice, tomatoes, cucumbers, onion, olives and tzatziki.

NOTE:

★ Omit pita bread and rice for low-carb, grain-free, and gluten-free options.

STICKY SESAME CHICKEN LEGS

PREP TIME: 5 MINUTES

COOK TIME: 20 MINUTES

TOTAL TIME: 25 MINUTES

COOK TEMPERATURE: 400°F

DIETARY CONSIDERATIONS:
EGG-FREE, NUT-FREE,
DAIRY-FREE

These are yummy, sticky, gooey, crispy chicken legs. Don't wear your new white shirt when you eat them, and be sure you have lots of napkins standing by!   **SERVINGS: 2**

- 4 chicken drumsticks
- 3 tablespoons soy sauce
- 2 tablespoons brown sugar
- 1 teaspoon minced garlic
- 1 teaspoon minced fresh ginger
- 1 teaspoon toasted sesame oil
- ½ teaspoon red pepper flakes
- ½ teaspoon kosher salt
- ½ teaspoon black pepper

1. Line a 7-inch round baking pan with aluminum foil. (If you don't do this, you'll either end up scrubbing forever or throwing out the pan.) Arrange the drumsticks in the prepared pan.

2. In a medium bowl, stir together the soy sauce, brown sugar, garlic, ginger, sesame oil, red pepper flakes, salt, and black pepper. Pour the sauce over the drumsticks and toss to coat.

3. Place the pan in the air-fryer basket. Set the air fryer to 400°F for 20 minutes, turning the drumsticks halfway through the cooking time. Use a meat thermometer to ensure the chicken has reached an internal temperature of 165°F. Serve immediately.

PECAN-CRUSTED CHICKEN TENDERS

These are kid-friendly chicken tenders that are easy to make and eat. The finer you crush the pecans, the easier time you'll have getting the pecans to stick to the tenders. Use coarse mustard for a full-bodied flavor. If you're allergic to mustard, you can always dip the tenders in a mixture of cream and honey and enjoy it that way.

SERVINGS: 4

PREP TIME: 5 MINUTES

COOK TIME: 12 MINUTES

TOTAL TIME: 17 MINUTES

COOK TEMPERATURE: 350°F

DIETARY CONSIDERATIONS: GRAIN-FREE, GLUTEN-FREE, SOY-FREE, DAIRY-FREE, PALEO*, LOW-CARB

1 pound chicken tenders

1 teaspoon kosher salt

1 teaspoon black pepper

½ teaspoon smoked paprika

¼ cup coarse mustard

2 tablespoons honey

1 cup finely crushed pecans (see Notes)

1. Place the chicken in a large bowl. Sprinkle with the salt, pepper, and paprika. Toss until the chicken is coated with the spices. Add the mustard and honey and toss until the chicken is coated.

2. Place the pecans on a plate. Working with one piece of chicken at a time, roll the chicken in the pecans until both sides are coated. Lightly brush off any loose pecans. Place the chicken in the air-fryer basket.

3. Set the air fryer to 350°F for 12 minutes, or until the chicken is cooked through and the pecans are golden brown.

NOTES:

★ If you allow honey in your Paleo diet, this recipe is Paleo compliant.

★ An easy way to crush the pecans is to place them in a resealable plastic bag and run a rolling pin over them until they're broken down to the desired consistency.

HERBED ROAST CHICKEN BREAST

If you find yourself too often reaching for rotisserie chicken at the grocery store, try this easy recipe at home. Two things are important: using a meat thermometer to get the cook time just right, and allowing the chicken to rest for a few minutes before slicing it (across the grain, of course). This is yet another good base recipe for making chicken breast in your air fryer, and it can be varied with any spice mix of your choice. Try the Lebanese Shawarma Spice Mix (page 183) for a change, or mix some yogurt and Garam Masala (page 181) for an Indian-inspired roast chicken.

SERVINGS: 2 TO 4

PREP TIME: 10 MINUTES

COOK TIME: 25 MINUTES

STANDING TIME: 5 MINUTES

TOTAL TIME: 40 MINUTES

COOK TEMPERATURE: 375°F

DIETARY CONSIDERATIONS: GRAIN-FREE, GLUTEN-FREE, EGG-FREE, NUT-FREE, SOY-FREE, PALEO, LOW-CARB

2 tablespoons salted butter or ghee (page 187), at room temperature

1 teaspoon dried Italian seasoning, crushed

½ teaspoon kosher salt

½ teaspoon smoked paprika

¼ teaspoon black pepper

2 bone-in, skin-on chicken breast halves (about 10 ounces each)

Lemon wedges, for serving

1. In a small bowl, stir together the butter, Italian seasoning, salt, paprika, and pepper until thoroughly combined.

2. Using a small sharp knife, carefully loosen the skin on each chicken breast half, starting at the thin end of each. Very carefully separate the skin from the flesh, leaving the skin attached at the thick end of each breast. Divide the herb butter into quarters. Rub one-quarter of the butter onto the flesh of each breast. Fold and lightly press the skin back onto each breast. Rub the remaining butter onto the skin of each breast.

3. Place the chicken in the air-fryer basket. Set the air fryer to 375°F for 25 minutes. Use a meat thermometer to ensure the chicken breasts have reached an internal temperature of 165°F.

4. Transfer the chicken to a cutting board. Lightly cover with aluminum foil and let rest for 5 to 10 minutes.

5. Serve with lemon wedges.

PERUVIAN-STYLE CHICKEN WITH GREEN HERB SAUCE

PREP TIME: 15 MINUTES

MARINATING TIME:
30 MINUTES

COOK TIME: 15 MINUTES

TOTAL TIME: 1 HOUR

COOK TEMPERATURE: 350°F

DIETARY CONSIDERATIONS:
GRAIN-FREE, GLUTEN-FREE,
EGG-FREE*, NUT-FREE,
SOY-FREE, DAIRY-FREE,
PALEO*, LOW-CARB

This yummy chicken is twice spiced—first with the marinade and then with the sauce. If you really wanted this to be authentic, you'd substitute a yellow ají amarillo for the serrano chile. But they're not easy to get, so I thought I'd offer you a substitute. You can also use a different chile paste, if you prefer.   **SERVINGS: 4**

For the Chicken

- 4 boneless, skinless chicken thighs (about 1½ pounds)
- 2 teaspoons grated lemon zest
- 2 tablespoons fresh lemon juice
- 1 tablespoon extra-virgin olive oil

- 1 serrano chile, seeded and minced
- 1 teaspoon ground cumin
- ½ teaspoon dried oregano, crushed
- ½ teaspoon kosher salt

For the Sauce

- 1 cup fresh cilantro leaves

- 1 jalapeño, seeded and coarsely chopped
- 1 garlic clove, minced
- 1 tablespoon extra-virgin olive oil
- 2½ teaspoons fresh lime juice
- ¼ teaspoon kosher salt
- ⅓ cup mayonnaise

1. **For the chicken:** Use a fork to pierce the chicken all over to allow the marinade to penetrate better. In a small bowl, combine the lemon zest, lemon juice, olive oil, serrano, cumin, oregano, and salt. Place the chicken in a large bowl or large resealable plastic bag. Pour the marinade over the chicken. Toss to coat. Marinate at room temperature for 30 minutes, or cover and refrigerate for up to 24 hours.

2. Place the chicken in the air-fryer basket. (Discard remaining marinade.) Set the air fryer to 350°F for 15 minutes, turning halfway through the cooking time.

3. **Meanwhile, for the sauce:** Combine the cilantro, jalapeño, garlic, olive oil, lime juice, and salt in a blender. Blend until combined. Add the mayonnaise and blend until pureed. Transfer to a small bowl. Cover and chill until ready to serve.

4. At the end of the cooking time, use a meat thermometer to ensure the chicken has reached an internal temperature of 165°F. Serve the chicken with the sauce.

NOTE:

★ If you eat Paleo, or are egg-free, use a compliant avocado oil-based mayonnaise.

SEAFOOD

SHRIMP SCAMPI

This was the first dish I made in the air fryer that required using a pan to cook something in the basket. Once I tried this, I was hooked and other ideas for air fryer recipes started to come to me. What I like about this is that it's one dish, no splatters to clean up, fairly hands-free, and fast. Many of my readers have told me this is the best shrimp scampi they've ever had.   **SERVINGS: 4**

PREP TIME: 8 MINUTES

COOK TIME: 8 MINUTES

TOTAL TIME: 16 MINUTES

COOK TEMPERATURE: 325°F

DIETARY CONSIDERATIONS:
GRAIN-FREE, GLUTEN-FREE,
EGG-FREE, NUT-FREE,
SOY-FREE, PALEO, LOW-CARB

4 tablespoons (½ stick) salted butter or ghee

1 tablespoon fresh lemon juice

1 tablespoon minced garlic

2 teaspoons red pepper flakes

1 pound shrimp (21 to 25 count), peeled and deveined

2 tablespoons chicken broth or dry white wine

2 tablespoons chopped fresh basil, plus more for sprinkling, or 1 teaspoon dried

1 tablespoon chopped fresh chives, or 1 teaspoon dried

1. Place a 7-inch round baking pan in the air-fryer basket. Set the air fryer to 325°F for 8 minutes (this will preheat the pan so the butter will melt faster).

2. Carefully remove the pan from the fryer and add the butter, lemon juice, garlic, and red pepper flakes. Place the pan back in the fryer.

3. Cook for 2 minutes, stirring once, until the butter has melted. (Do not skip this step; this is what infuses the butter with garlic flavor, which is what makes it all taste so good.)

4. Carefully remove the pan from the fryer and add the shrimp, broth, basil, and chives. Stir gently until the ingredients are well combined.

5. Return the pan to the air fryer and cook for 5 minutes, stirring once.

6. Thoroughly stir the shrimp mixture and let it rest for 1 minute on a wire rack. (This is so the shrimp cooks in the residual heat rather than getting overcooked and rubbery.)

7. Stir once more, sprinkle with additional chopped fresh basil, and serve.

TILAPIA ALMONDINE

Let's all admit it—we each have things we love that we're told we should be too snobbish to love. For me, it is this baked fish from a local cafeteria (I know, gasp!). But as a busy mom, sometimes the best way to feed the kids meat and veggies was to duck into this cafeteria near our house, pick up this dish, and ensure that each of us got what we wanted. I sometimes crave that fish, even though the cafeteria seems to have disappeared. Make this super-simple but flavorful recipe, and you, too, might start to crave it all too often. **SERVINGS: 2**

PREP TIME: 10 MINUTES

COOK TIME: 10 MINUTES

TOTAL TIME: 20 MINUTES

COOK TEMPERATURE: 325°F

DIETARY CONSIDERATIONS: GRAIN-FREE, GLUTEN-FREE, EGG-FREE*, SOY-FREE, PALEO*, LOW-CARB

½ cup almond flour or fine dried bread crumbs

2 tablespoons salted butter or ghee, melted

1 teaspoon black pepper

½ teaspoon kosher salt

¼ cup mayonnaise

2 tilapia fillets

½ cup thinly sliced almonds

Vegetable oil spray

1. In a small bowl, mix together the almond flour, butter, pepper and salt.

2. Spread the mayonnaise on both sides of each fish fillet. Dredge the fillets in the almond flour mixture. Spread the sliced almonds on one side of each fillet, pressing lightly to adhere.

3. Spray the air-fryer basket with vegetable oil spray. Place the fish fillets in the basket. Set the air fryer to 325°F for 10 minutes, or until the fish flakes easily with a fork.

NOTE:

★ If you eat Paleo, or are egg-free, use a compliant avocado oil-based mayonnaise.

DUKKAH-CRUSTED HALIBUT

Dukkah is a great, aromatic, nutty, flavorful mix of various nuts and spices. This recipe is a testament to my lazy/efficient style. Not only do I make my dukkah with roasted mixed nuts, thereby skipping having to roast a bunch of nuts separately, but I also toast the seeds in the air fryer itself. If you've ever tried toasting sesame seeds, you know how they love to leap out of the saucepan and say hello to your face. Toasting them in the air fryer keeps your face safe while still getting the seeds well toasted. Sprinkle leftover dukkah over steamed vegetables or mix it with oil and serve it as a dip for pita. **SERVINGS: 2**

PREP TIME: 15 MINUTES

COOK TIME: 17 MINUTES

TOTAL TIME: 32 MINUTES

COOK TEMPERATURE: 400°F

DIETARY CONSIDERATIONS:
GRAIN-FREE, GLUTEN-FREE,
EGG-FREE*, SOY-FREE,
DAIRY-FREE, PALEO*,
LOW-CARB

For the Dukkah

- 1 **tablespoon coriander seeds**
- 1 **tablespoon sesame seeds**
- 1½ **teaspoons cumin seeds**
- ⅓ **cup roasted mixed nuts**
- ¼ **teaspoon kosher salt**
- ¼ **teaspoon black pepper**

For the Fish

- 2 **(5-ounce) halibut fillets**
- 2 **tablespoons mayonnaise**
- **Vegetable oil spray**
- **Lemon wedges, for serving**

1. **For the dukkah:** Combine the coriander, sesame seeds, and cumin in a small baking pan. Place the pan in the air-fryer basket. Set the air fryer to 400°F for 5 minutes. Toward the end of the cooking time, you will hear the seeds popping. Transfer to a plate and let cool for 5 minutes.

2. Transfer the toasted seeds to a food processor or spice grinder and add the mixed nuts. Pulse until coarsely chopped. Add the salt and pepper and stir well.

3. **For the fish:** Spread each fillet with 1 tablespoon of the mayonnaise. Press a heaping tablespoon of the dukkah into the mayonnaise on each fillet, pressing lightly to adhere.

4. Spray the air-fryer basket with vegetable oil spray. Place the fish in the basket. Set the air fryer to 400°F for 12 minutes, or until the fish flakes easily with a fork.

5. Serve the fish with lemon wedges.

NOTE:

★ If you eat Paleo or are egg-free, use a compliant avocado oil-based mayonnaise.

BAKED SHRIMP CURRY

Yet another weird but wonderful recipe that only came about because I was being lazy and didn't want to wash too many dishes. I marinated some shrimp in a coconut milk mixture and then, being frugal as I am, decided to just cook it, marinade and all. I was quite sure the marinade would mostly evaporate, but lucky for us, I was wrong. What resulted was a baked shrimp curry that is as wonderful as it is weird-sounding. In fact, you may want to use it for the Crispy Cracked-Pepper Chicken Wings (page 66) as well. **SERVINGS: 4**

PREP TIME: 10 MINUTES

MARINATING TIME:
30 MINUTES

COOK TIME: 10 MINUTES

TOTAL TIME: 50 MINUTES

COOK TEMPERATURE: 375°F

DIETARY CONSIDERATIONS:
GRAIN-FREE, GLUTEN-FREE,
EGG-FREE, NUT-FREE,
SOY-FREE, DAIRY-FREE,
PALEO, LOW-CARB

¾ cup unsweetened full-fat coconut milk

¼ cup finely chopped yellow onion

2 teaspoons Garam Masala (page 181)

1 tablespoon minced fresh ginger

1 tablespoon minced garlic

1 teaspoon ground turmeric

1 teaspoon salt

¼ to ½ teaspoon cayenne pepper

1 pound raw shrimp (21 to 25 count), peeled and deveined

2 teaspoons chopped fresh cilantro

1. In a large bowl, stir together the coconut milk, onion, garam masala, ginger, garlic, turmeric, salt and cayenne, until well blended.

2. Add the shrimp and toss until coated with sauce on all sides. Marinate at room temperature for 30 minutes.

3. Transfer the shrimp and marinade to a 7-inch round baking pan with 4-inch sides. Place the pan in the air-fryer basket. Set the air fryer to 375°F for 10 minutes, stirring halfway through the cooking time.

4. Transfer the shrimp to a serving bowl or platter. Sprinkle with the cilantro and serve.

CRISPY SALT-&-PEPPER SHRIMP

I tried three or four different coatings before I settled on rice flour for this recipe. I realized it makes the best, lightest, and crunchiest coating. I know it's not something all of us always have in our pantries, but it's inexpensive and totally worth it. You may find yourself breading chicken tenders and other goodies with it as well.

SERVINGS: 4

PREP TIME: 10 MINUTES

COOK TIME: 8 MINUTES

TOTAL TIME: 18 MINUTES

COOK TEMPERATURE: 325°F

DIETARY CONSIDERATIONS: GLUTEN-FREE, EGG-FREE, NUT-FREE, SOY-FREE, DAIRY-FREE

2 teaspoons whole black peppercorns

2 teaspoons Sichuan peppercorns

1 teaspoon kosher salt

1 teaspoon sugar

1 pound raw shrimp (21 to 25 count), peeled and deveined

3 tablespoons rice flour

2 tablespoons vegetable oil

Vegetable oil spray

1. In a small heavy-bottomed skillet, toast the black peppercorns and Sichuan peppercorns over medium heat, stirring frequently, until fragrant, 1 to 2 minutes. Let cool completely.

2. Transfer the peppercorns to a mortar. Add the salt and sugar. Use the pestle to crush the spices into a coarse powder.

3. Place the shrimp in a large bowl. Sprinkle with the spice mixture, rice flour, and vegetable oil. Toss until the shrimp are evenly coated.

4. Place the shrimp in the air-fryer basket, trying to keep them in as flat a layer as possible. (You may want to use a rack—place half the shrimp in the basket and half on the rack.) Spray generously with vegetable oil spray. Set the air fryer to 325°F for 8 minutes, tossing the shrimp halfway through the cooking time, until the shrimp are cooked through and have a lightly browned and crisp exterior crust. If not, cook for 1 to 2 minutes more.

CRUSTLESS SHRIMP QUICHE

Here's a great base recipe that you can make with shrimp, crabmeat, or even cooked chicken, but the shrimp version is my favorite. I really love being able to cook raw shrimp gently but perfectly in the air fryer. This makes a great breakfast or brunch dish. Just be sure to grease the pan really, really well. If you have a pan with a removable bottom or a springform pan that fits in your air fryer, it would be perfect for this dish, allowing you to unmold a flawless masterpiece before serving.   **SERVINGS: 2**

PREP TIME: 15 MINUTES

COOK TIME: 20 MINUTES

TOTAL TIME: 35 MINUTES

COOK TEMPERATURE: 300°F

DIETARY CONSIDERATIONS: GRAIN-FREE, GLUTEN-FREE, NUT-FREE, SOY-FREE, LOW-CARB

Vegetable oil

4   large eggs

½   cup half-and-half

4   ounces raw shrimp, chopped (about 1 cup)

1   cup shredded Parmesan or Swiss cheese

¼   cup chopped scallions

1   teaspoon sweet smoked paprika

1   teaspoon herbes de Provence

1   teaspoon black pepper

½ to 1   teaspoon kosher salt

1. Generously grease a 7-inch round baking pan with 4-inch sides with vegetable oil. (Be sure to grease the pan well—the proteins in eggs stick something fierce. Alternatively, line the bottom of the pan with parchment paper cut to fit and spray the parchment and sides of the pan generously with vegetable oil spray.)

2. In a large bowl, beat together the eggs and half-and-half. Add the shrimp, ¾ cup of the cheese, the scallions, paprika, herbes de Provence, pepper, and salt. Stir with a fork to thoroughly combine. Pour the egg mixture into the prepared pan.

3. Place the pan in the air-fryer basket. Set the air fryer to 300°F for 20 minutes. After 17 minutes, sprinkle the remaining ¼ cup cheese on top and cook for the remaining 3 minutes, or until the cheese has melted, the eggs are set, and a toothpick inserted into the center comes out clean.

4. Serve the quiche warm or at room temperature.

VARIATIONS TO TRY:
★ Substitute cheddar or Swiss cheese for the Parmesan.
★ Add goat cheese or feta cheese for tanginess.
★ Add ½ cup chopped cooked bacon.
★ Substitute red or white onions for the scallions.
★ Substitute diced broccoli for the scallions.
★ Substitute dried Italian or Greek herb blend for the herbes de Provence.
★ Use heavy cream instead of half-and-half.
★ Use a mix of crabmeat and chopped raw shrimp.

MISO SALMON

Miso salmon seems to be all the range in high-end restaurants these days, and with good reason. But the beauty of this dish is that it takes almost nothing to prepare at home. The little bit of sugar in the glaze really helps create a lovely caramelized finish, and also contrasts very well with the salty flavor of the miso.

SERVINGS: 2

PREP TIME: 10 MINUTES

COOK TIME: 12 MINUTES

TOTAL TIME: 22 MINUTES

COOK TEMPERATURE: 400°F

DIETARY CONSIDERATIONS: EGG-FREE, DAIRY-FREE, NUT-FREE

2 tablespoons brown sugar

2 tablespoons soy sauce

2 tablespoons white miso paste

1 teaspoon minced garlic

1 teaspoon minced fresh ginger

½ teaspoon freshly cracked black pepper

2 (5-ounce) salmon fillets

Vegetable oil spray

1 teaspoon sesame seeds

2 scallions, thinly sliced, for garnish

1. In a small bowl, whisk together the brown sugar, soy sauce, miso, garlic, ginger, and pepper to combine.

2. Place the salmon fillets on a plate. Pour half the sauce over the fillets; turn the fillets to coat the other sides with sauce.

3. Spray the air-fryer basket with vegetable oil spray. Place the sauce-covered salmon in the basket. Set the air fryer to 400°F for 12 minutes. Halfway through the cooking time, brush additional miso sauce on the salmon.

4. Sprinkle the salmon with the sesame seeds and scallions and serve.

CITRUS-SOY SALMON WITH SESAME BOK CHOY & SHIITAKES

The orange juice and soy sauce in this marinade make a lovely salty-sweet combination. And the air fryer does an impressive job of browning the salmon so that you can present a beautiful piece of fish at the table with very little effort. You can use any other firm, slightly fatty fish as a substitute for the salmon.   **SERVINGS: 2**

PREP TIME: 15 MINUTES

MARINATING TIME: 30 MINUTES

COOK TIME: 12 MINUTES

TOTAL TIME: 57 MINUTES

COOK TEMPERATURE: 400°F

DIETARY CONSIDERATIONS: NUT-FREE, EGG-FREE, DAIRY-FREE, LOW-CARB

For the Fish

- ½ cup fresh orange juice
- ¼ cup soy sauce
- 3 tablespoons rice vinegar
- 2 garlic cloves, minced
- 1 tablespoon minced fresh ginger
- 1 tablespoon vegetable oil
- 2 teaspoons finely grated orange zest
- ½ teaspoon kosher salt
- 2 (5- to 6-ounce) salmon fillets

For the Vegetables

- 2 heads baby bok choy, halved lengthwise
- 2 ounces shiitake mushrooms, stemmed
- 1 tablespoon toasted sesame oil

  Kosher salt
- ½ teaspoon sesame seeds, toasted

1. **For the fish:** In a small bowl, whisk together the orange juice, soy sauce, vinegar, garlic, ginger, vegetable oil, orange zest, and salt. Set aside half the marinade. Place the salmon in a gallon-size resealable bag. Pour the remaining marinade over the salmon. Seal and massage to coat. Let stand at room temperature for 30 minutes.

2. Place the salmon in the air-fryer basket. (Discard marinade.) Set the air fryer to 400°F for 12 minutes.

3. **Meanwhile, for the vegetables:** Brush the bok choy and mushroom caps all over with the sesame oil and season lightly with salt.

4. After the salmon has cooked for 6 minutes, add the vegetables around the salmon in the air-fryer basket. Cook for the remaining 6 minutes.

5. To serve, drizzle the salmon with some of the reserved marinade and sprinkle the vegetables with the sesame seeds.

SMOKY SHRIMP & CHORIZO TAPAS

PREP TIME: 15 MINUTES

COOK TIME: 10 MINUTES

TOTAL TIME: 25 MINUTES

COOK TEMPERATURE: 375°F

DIETARY CONSIDERATIONS:
EGG-FREE, NUT-FREE,
SOY-FREE, LOW-CARB,
GRAIN-FREE, GLUTEN-FREE

I first had this in Brazil—I know, I know, that doesn't make sense. But we went to a fabulous tapas place in São Paulo and fell in love with these shrimp and chorizo tapas. It's a great combination, especially with the paprika—a little taste of Spain in your own kitchen.   **SERVINGS: 2 TO 4**

4 ounces Spanish (cured) chorizo, halved horizontally and sliced crosswise (see Note)

½ pound raw medium shrimp, peeled and deveined

1 tablespoon extra-virgin olive oil

1 small shallot, halved and thinly sliced

1 garlic clove, minced

1 tablespoon finely chopped fresh oregano

½ teaspoon smoked Spanish paprika

¼ teaspoon kosher salt

¼ teaspoon black pepper

3 tablespoons fresh orange juice

1 tablespoon minced fresh parsley

1. Place the chorizo in a 7-inch round baking pan with 4-inch sides. Set the pan in the air-fryer basket. Set the air fryer to 375°F for 5 minutes, or until the chorizo has started to brown and render its fat.

2. Meanwhile, in a large bowl, combine the shrimp, olive oil, shallot, garlic, oregano, paprika, salt, and pepper. Toss until the shrimp is well coated.

3. Transfer the shrimp to the pan with the chorizo. Stir to combine. Place the pan in the air-fryer basket. Cook for 10 minutes, stirring halfway through the cooking time.

4. Transfer the shrimp and chorizo to a serving dish. Drizzle with the orange juice and toss to combine. Sprinkle with the parsley.

NOTE:

★ Spanish chorizo is a hard, cured sausage, as opposed to Mexican chorizo, which is fresh. If you can't find it, substitute 4 ounces bulk Mexican chorizo, broken into small pieces.

SPICY CRAB CAKES WITH MANGO MAYO

You know those super-simple premade crab cakes you can buy at the grocery store? Yeah, don't buy those. Make your own. So much better! More crab, fewer fillers, and cheaper by far than the store-bought kind. And that warm mango mayo? You'll be making it again and again, to serve with just about everything.

SERVINGS: 4

PREP TIME: 25 MINUTES

COOK TIME: 15 MINUTES

TOTAL TIME: 40 MINUTES

COOK TEMPERATURE: 375°F

DIETARY CONSIDERATIONS: NUT-FREE, DAIRY-FREE, SOY-FREE

For the Crab Cakes

- ½ cup chopped red onion
- ½ cup fresh cilantro leaves
- 1 small serrano chile or jalapeño, seeded and quartered
- ½ pound lump crabmeat
- 1 large egg
- 1 tablespoon mayonnaise
- 1 tablespoon whole-grain mustard
- 2 teaspoons minced fresh ginger
- ½ teaspoon ground cumin
- ½ teaspoon ground coriander
- ¼ teaspoon kosher salt
- 2 tablespoons fresh lemon juice
- 1½ cups panko bread crumbs
- Vegetable oil spray

For the Mango Mayo

- ½ cup diced fresh mango
- ½ cup mayonnaise
- ½ teaspoon grated lime zest
- 2 teaspoons fresh lime juice
- Pinch of cayenne pepper

1. **For the crab cakes:** Combine the onion, cilantro, and serrano in a food processor. Pulse until minced.

2. In a large bowl, combine the minced vegetable mixture with the crabmeat, egg, mayonnaise, mustard, ginger, cumin, coriander, and salt. Add the lemon juice and mix gently until thoroughly combined. Add 1 cup of the bread crumbs. Mix gently again until well blended.

3. Form into four evenly sized patties. Put the remaining ½ cup bread crumbs in a shallow bowl and press both sides of each patty into the bread crumbs.

4. Arrange the patties in the air-fryer basket. Spray with vegetable oil spray. Set the air fryer to 375°F for 15 minutes, turning and spraying other side of the patties with vegetable oil spray halfway through the cooking time, until the crab cakes are golden brown and crisp.

5. **Meanwhile, for the mayonnaise:** In a blender, combine the mango, mayonnaise, lime zest, lime juice, and cayenne. Blend until smooth.

6. Serve the crab cakes warm, with the mango mayo.

SPICY CAJUN FISH FILLETS

I've given you a simple and tasty Cajun spice mix here, but you can always buy a mix, if you prefer. It is, however, but the work of a moment to make this blend, and it tastes fresh and a lot better than what you can get in most stores. The spice recipe makes about 4 tablespoons. I used about 1 tablespoon for 2 fish fillets. If your air fryer will hold more fish than that, you can always double the recipe. But as fast as they cook, you could cook in two batches and still have dinner made quickly.   **SERVINGS: 2**

PREP TIME: 10 MINUTES

COOK TIME: 8 MINUTES

TOTAL TIME: 20 MINUTES

COOK TEMPERATURE: 400°F

DIETARY CONSIDERATIONS:
GRAIN-FREE, GLUTEN-FREE,
EGG-FREE, NUT-FREE,
SOY-FREE, DAIRY-FREE,
LOW-CARB

For the Cajun Spice Mix*

- 1 teaspoon dried oregano
- 1 teaspoon dried thyme
- 1 tablespoon dried parsley flakes
- 1 tablespoon dehydrated minced onion

- 1 teaspoon dehydrated minced garlic
- 1 tablespoon smoked paprika
- 1 teaspoon cayenne pepper
- 1 teaspoon black pepper
- 1 teaspoon kosher salt

For the Fish

Vegetable oil spray

- 2 firm white-fleshed fish fillets, such as cod, haddock, catfish, flounder, grouper, or sea bass (about 5 ounces each)
- ½ lemon, cut into 2 wedges

1. **For the Cajun spice mix:** In a spice or coffee grinder, combine the oregano, thyme, parsley, onion, garlic, paprika, cayenne, black pepper, and salt. Pulse a few times to combine.

2. **For the fish:** Spray the fish fillets with vegetable oil spray on both sides. Divide 1 tablespoon of spice mix evenly between the two fillets, working it gently into the fish with your fingers, ensuring the fish is evenly covered.

3. Place the fish in the air-fryer basket. Spray with vegetable oil spray again. (White-fleshed fish is lean and can get dry, so don't skimp on the oil.) Set the air fryer to 400°F for 8 minutes, spraying the fish with vegetable oil spray again halfway through the cooking time.

4. Serve with the lemon wedges.

NOTE:

★ This makes about 4 tablespoons spice mix. Store leftovers in a tightly sealed container in a cool, dark place. Stir or shake before using.

SHRIMP WITH SMOKY TOMATO DRESSING

I made this super-simple recipe two ways: I cooked it in the sauce in one version, and without the sauce in the next. Take my word for this—cook it with the sauce. It's a little messier to clean up, but heating that sauce makes it all kinds of delicious. I love how easily it all comes together. You can serve this with steamed rice or steamed bok choy as a main dish. If you want to serve it as an appetizer, definitely leave the tails on the shrimp so you can use them to pick up the shrimp and just pop them into your mouths—more fun to eat them that way! **SERVINGS: 2**

PREP TIME: 5 MINUTES

COOK TIME: 8 MINUTES

TOTAL TIME: 13 MINUTES

COOK TEMPERATURE: 350°F

DIETARY CONSIDERATIONS:
GRAIN-FREE, GLUTEN-FREE,
NUT-FREE, SOY-FREE,
DAIRY-FREE, LOW-CARB

3 tablespoons mayonnaise

1 tablespoon ketchup

1 tablespoon minced garlic

1 teaspoon sriracha

½ teaspoon smoked paprika

½ teaspoon kosher salt

1 pound large raw shrimp (21 to 25 count), peeled (tails left on) and deveined

Vegetable oil spray

½ cup chopped scallions

1. In a large bowl, combine the mayonnaise, ketchup, garlic, sriracha, paprika, and salt. Add the shrimp and toss to coat with the sauce.

2. Spray the air-fryer basket with vegetable oil spray. Place the shrimp in the basket. Set the air fryer to 350°F for 8 minutes, tossing and spraying the shrimp with vegetable oil spray halfway through the cooking time.

3. Sprinkle with the chopped scallions before serving.

SCALLOPS & SPINACH WITH TOMATO-BASIL CREAM SAUCE

This recipe is perfect for date night. I use jumbo sea scallops, and while they're not cheap, it's still a lot more economical to make them at home. Let me tell you—had you been served these scallops at a fine restaurant, you would have had no complaints. Don't let the simple list of ingredients deceive you. Creamy tomato-basil sauce and spinach form the perfect accompaniment to scallops. Serve with steamed rice to complete the meal. **SERVINGS: 2**

PREP TIME: 5 MINUTES

COOK TIME: 10 MINUTES

TOTAL TIME: 15 MINUTES

COOK TEMPERATURE: 350°F

DIETARY CONSIDERATIONS: GRAIN-FREE, GLUTEN-FREE, EGG-FREE, NUT-FREE, SOY-FREE, LOW-CARB

Vegetable oil spray

1 (10-ounce) package frozen spinach, thawed and drained

8 jumbo sea scallops

Kosher salt and black pepper

¾ cup heavy cream

1 tablespoon tomato paste

1 tablespoon chopped fresh basil

1 teaspoon minced garlic

1. Spray a 7-inch round baking pan with vegetable oil spray. Spread the thawed spinach in an even layer in the bottom of the pan.

2. Spray both sides of the scallops with vegetable oil spray. Season lightly with salt and pepper. Arrange the scallops on top of the spinach.

3. In a small bowl, whisk together the cream, tomato paste, basil, garlic, ½ teaspoon salt, and ½ teaspoon pepper. Pour the sauce over the scallops and spinach.

4. Place the pan in the air-fryer basket. Set the air fryer to 350°F for 10 minutes. Use a meat thermometer to ensure the scallops have an internal temperature of 130°F.

LEMON-TARRAGON FISH EN PAPILLOTE

This is one of those dishes that is so easy to make but looks so utterly elegant. Those tempting aromas that waft up as diners wonder what's inside the packets and the reveal when they finally peek inside make dinnertime fun and surprising. **SERVINGS: 2**

PREP TIME: 10 MINUTES

COOK TIME: 15 MINUTES

TOTAL TIME: 25 MINUTES

COOK TEMPERATURE: 350°F

DIETARY CONSIDERATIONS: GRAIN-FREE, GLUTEN-FREE, EGG-FREE, NUT-FREE, SOY-FREE, LOW-CARB

- 2 tablespoons salted butter, melted
- 1 tablespoon fresh lemon juice
- ½ teaspoon dried tarragon, crushed, or 2 sprigs fresh tarragon (see Note)
- 1 teaspoon kosher salt
- ½ cup julienned carrots
- ½ cup julienned fennel, or ¼ cup julienned celery
- ½ cup thinly sliced red bell pepper
- 2 (6-ounce) cod fillets, thawed if frozen
- Vegetable oil spray
- ½ teaspoon black pepper

1. In a medium bowl, combine the butter, lemon juice, tarragon, and ½ teaspoon of the salt. Whisk well until you get a creamy sauce. Add the carrots, fennel, and bell pepper and toss to combine; set aside.

2. Cut two squares of parchment each large enough to hold one fillet and half the vegetables. Spray the fillets with vegetable oil spray. Season both sides with the remaining ½ teaspoon salt and the black pepper.

3. Lay one fillet down on each parchment square. Top each with half the vegetables. Pour any remaining sauce over the vegetables.

4. Fold over the parchment paper and crimp the sides in small, tight folds to hold the fish, vegetables, and sauce securely inside the packet. Place the packets in the air-fryer basket. Set the air fryer to 350°F for 15 minutes.

5. Transfer each packet to a plate. Cut open with scissors just before serving (be careful, as the steam inside will be hot).

NOTE:

★ If you are using fresh tarragon, leave it out of the butter mixture and instead place 1 sprig on top of the vegetables in each packet right before sealing the packet.

BEEF, PORK & LAMB

CARNE ASADA

I know someone will want to yank my Texan card for making carne asada in the air fryer rather than on the grill, but that's probably only until they try this recipe. This is the real deal, and for those times when you can't grill outside or just want a quick meal, use your air fryer and enjoy! I serve mine with Mexican rice and refried beans made in the pressure cooker, or use as filling for tacos along with red onions, cilantro, guacamole, and corn tortillas. **SERVINGS: 4**

PREP TIME: 10 MINUTES

MARINATING TIME:
30 MINUTES

COOK TIME: 8 MINUTES

TOTAL TIME: 48 MINUTES

COOK TEMPERATURE: 400°F

DIETARY CONSIDERATIONS:
GRAIN-FREE, GLUTEN-FREE,
EGG-FREE, NUT-FREE,
SOY-FREE, DAIRY-FREE,
LOW-CARB

Juice of 2 limes

1 orange, peeled and seeded

1 cup fresh cilantro leaves

1 jalapeño, diced

2 tablespoons vegetable oil

2 tablespoons apple cider vinegar

2 teaspoons ancho chile powder

2 teaspoons sugar

1 teaspoon kosher salt

1 teaspoon cumin seeds

1 teaspoon coriander seeds

1½ pounds skirt steak, cut into 3 pieces

1. In a blender, combine the lime juice, orange, cilantro, jalapeño, vegetable oil, vinegar, chile powder, sugar, salt, cumin, and coriander. Blend until smooth.

2. Place the steak in a resealable plastic bag. Pour the marinade over the steak and seal the bag. Let stand at room temperature for 30 minutes or cover and refrigerate for up to 24 hours.

3. Place the steak pieces in the air-fryer basket (depending on the size of your air fryer, you may have to do this in two batches). Discard marinade. Set the air fryer to 400°F for 8 minutes. Use a meat thermometer to ensure the steak has reached an internal temperature of 145°F. (It is critical to not overcook skirt steak to avoid toughening the meat.)

4. Transfer the steak to a cutting board and let rest for 10 minutes. Slice across the grain and serve.

EASY BEEF SATAY

I love making satay at home because not only is it easy, but you can pig out and make as many as your air fryer will hold. No more rationing the two to four little skewers you get at restaurants among all of you. Eat up! I love mine with lots of crushed peanuts sprinkled on top.   **SERVINGS: 4**

PREP TIME: 10 MINUTES

MARINATING TIME:
30 MINUTES

COOK TIME: 8 MINUTES

TOTAL TIME: 48 MINUTES

COOK TEMPERATURE: 400°F

DIETARY CONSIDERATIONS:
EGG-FREE, DAIRY-FREE,
LOW-CARB

- 1 **pound beef flank steak, thinly sliced into long strips**
- 2 **tablespoons vegetable oil**
- 1 **tablespoon fish sauce**
- 1 **tablespoon soy sauce**
- 1 **tablespoon minced fresh ginger**
- 1 **tablespoon minced garlic**
- 1 **tablespoon sugar**
- 1 **teaspoon sriracha or other hot sauce**
- 1 **teaspoon ground coriander**
- ½ **cup chopped fresh cilantro**
- ¼ **cup chopped roasted peanuts**

  Easy Peanut Sauce (page 185), for serving

1. Place the beef strips in a large bowl or resealable plastic bag. Add the vegetable oil, fish sauce, soy sauce, ginger, garlic, sugar, sriracha, coriander, and ¼ cup of the cilantro to the bag. Seal and massage the bag to thoroughly coat and combine. Marinate at room temperature for 30 minutes, or cover and refrigerate for up to 24 hours.

2. Using tongs, remove the beef strips from the bag and lay them flat in the air-fryer basket, minimizing overlap as much as possible; discard the marinade. Set the air fryer to 400°F for 8 minutes, turning the beef strips halfway through the cooking time.

3. Transfer the meat to a serving platter. Sprinkle with the remaining ¼ cup cilantro and the peanuts. Serve with peanut sauce.

BULGOGI BURGERS

Yet another use for gochujang (Korean red chile paste), which is among my favorite seasonings, in this Korean-inspired dish, which is one of all-time favorite cuisines. But most important, this is yet another way to make burgers that your whole family will enjoy. Serve them with hamburger buns or, for a change, serve with large lettuce leaves for a combination of hot and cold and crunchy that's to die for.

SERVINGS: 4

PREP TIME: 15 MINUTES

MARINATING TIME: 30 MINUTES

COOK TIME: 10 MINUTES

TOTAL TIME: 55 MINUTES

COOK TEMPERATURE: 350°F

DIETARY CONSIDERATIONS: NUT-FREE, DAIRY-FREE

For the Burgers

- 1 pound 85% lean ground beef
- ¼ cup chopped scallions
- 2 tablespoons gochujang (Korean red chile paste)
- 1 tablespoon dark soy sauce
- 2 teaspoons minced garlic
- 2 teaspoons minced fresh ginger
- 2 teaspoons sugar
- 1 tablespoon toasted sesame oil
- ½ teaspoon kosher salt

For the Gochujang Mayonnaise

- ¼ cup mayonnaise
- ¼ cup chopped scallions
- 1 tablespoon gochujang (Korean red chile paste)
- 1 tablespoon toasted sesame oil
- 2 teaspoons sesame seeds
- 4 hamburger buns

1. **For the burgers:** In a large bowl, mix the ground beef, scallions, gochujang, soy sauce, garlic, ginger, sugar, sesame oil, and salt. Marinate at room temperature for 30 minutes, or cover and refrigerate for up to 24 hours.

2. Divide the meat into four portions and form them into round patties. Make a slight depression in the middle of each patty with your thumb to prevent them from puffing up into a dome shape while cooking.

3. Place the patties in a single layer in the air-fryer basket. Set the air fryer to 350°F for 10 minutes.

4. **Meanwhile, for the gochujang mayonnaise:** Stir together the mayonnaise, scallions, gochujang, sesame oil, and sesame seeds.

5. At the end of the cooking time, use a meat thermometer to ensure the burgers have reached an internal temperature of 160°F (medium).

6. To serve, place the burgers on the buns and top with the mayonnaise.

CANTONESE BBQ PORK (CHAR SIU)

For this recipe, I ask you to make twice as much marinade as you'll need for the pork. This is because air fryers need the surface area of the meat you're cooking to be somewhat dry for best results. But I like my char siu saucy—just like me—so I cook down the extra marinade to get a lovely glaze or dip for the cooked char siu. **SERVINGS: 4**

PREP TIME: 10 MINUTES

MARINATING TIME:
30 MINUTES

COOK TIME: 15 MINUTES

TOTAL TIME: 55 MINUTES

COOK TEMPERATURE: 400°F

DIETARY CONSIDERATIONS:
DAIRY-FREE, EGG-FREE,
NUT-FREE

¼ cup honey

2 tablespoons dark soy sauce

1 tablespoon sugar

1 tablespoon Shaoxing wine (rice cooking wine)

1 tablespoon hoisin sauce

2 teaspoons minced garlic

2 teaspoons minced fresh ginger

1 teaspoon Chinese five-spice powder

1 pound fatty pork shoulder, cut into long, 1-inch-thick pieces

1. In a small microwave-safe bowl, combine the honey, soy sauce, sugar, wine, hoisin, garlic, ginger, and five-spice powder. Microwave in 10-second intervals, stirring in between, until the honey has dissolved.

2. Use a fork to pierce the pork slices to allow the marinade to penetrate better. Place the pork in a large bowl or resealable plastic bag and pour in half the marinade; set aside the remaining marinade to use for the sauce. Toss to coat. Marinate the pork at room temperature for 30 minutes, or cover and refrigerate for up 24 hours.

3. Place the pork in a single layer in the air-fryer basket. Set the air fryer to 400°F for 15 minutes, turning and basting the pork halfway through the cooking time.

4. While the pork is cooking, microwave the reserved marinade on high for 45 to 60 seconds, stirring every 15 seconds, to thicken it slightly to the consistency of a sauce. (Because it has honey in it, be careful not to overcook it, or you'll have char siu toffee—ask me how I know.)

5. Transfer the pork to a cutting board and let rest for 10 minutes. Brush with the sauce and serve.

CHINESE-STYLE BABY BACK RIBS

I love the way the sauce sticks to the ribs and caramelizes right on them. Sticky, meaty goodness, y'all, and perfectly messy and lovely to eat. You may need to adjust the cooking time depending on how thick your ribs are. A meat thermometer will be your friend. Serve as an appetizer, or alongside some plain steamed rice and a veggie for a meal. **SERVINGS: 4**

PREP TIME: 10 MINUTES

MARINATING TIME: 30 MINUTES

COOK TIME: 30 MINUTES

TOTAL TIME: 1 HOUR 10 MINUTES

COOK TEMPERATURE: 350°F

DIETARY CONSIDERATIONS: EGG-FREE, NUT-FREE, DAIRY-FREE, LOW-CARB

1 tablespoon toasted sesame oil

1 tablespoon fermented black bean paste

1 tablespoon Shaoxing wine (rice cooking wine)

1 tablespoon dark soy sauce

1 tablespoon agave nectar or honey

1 teaspoon minced garlic

1 teaspoon minced fresh ginger

1 (1½-pound) slab baby back ribs, cut into individual ribs

1. In a large bowl, stir together the sesame oil, black bean paste, wine, soy sauce, agave, garlic, and ginger. Add the ribs and toss well to coat. Marinate at room temperature for 30 minutes, or cover and refrigerate for up to 24 hours.

2. Place the ribs in the air-fryer basket; discard the marinade. Set the air fryer to 350°F for 30 minutes.

PORK BULGOGI (DAE JI BULGOGI)

I love a good pork bulgogi, and I've made this every which way, including in a pressure cooker (yum!). But the crispiness and caramelizing you get with an air fryer is just perfect. You can make the marinade ahead of time and use it when you're ready to marinate the pork, since it will keep well in the refrigerator for at least a week.

SERVINGS: 4

PREP TIME: 10 MINUTES

MARINATING TIME: 30 MINUTES

COOK TIME: 15 MINUTES

TOTAL TIME: 55 MINUTES

COOK TEMPERATURE: 400°F

DIETARY CONSIDERATIONS: EGG-FREE, NUT-FREE, DAIRY-FREE

- 1 onion, thinly sliced
- 2 tablespoons gochujang (Korean red chile paste)
- 1 tablespoon minced fresh ginger
- 1 tablespoon minced garlic
- 1 tablespoon soy sauce
- 1 tablespoon Shaoxing wine (rice cooking wine)
- 1 tablespoon toasted sesame oil
- 1 teaspoon sugar
- ¼ to 1 teaspoon cayenne pepper or gochugaru (Korean ground red pepper)
- 1 pound boneless pork shoulder, cut into ½-inch-thick slices
- 1 tablespoon sesame seeds
- ¼ cup sliced scallions

1. In a large bowl, combine the onion, gochujang, ginger, garlic, soy sauce, wine, sesame oil, sugar, and cayenne. Add the pork and toss to coat. Marinate at room temperature for 30 minutes, or cover and refrigerate for up to 24 hours.

2. Arrange the pork and onion slices in the air-fryer basket; discard the marinade. Set the air fryer to 400°F for 15 minutes, turning the pork halfway through the cooking time.

3. Arrange the pork on a serving platter. Sprinkle with the sesame seeds and scallions and serve.

INDIAN MINT & CHILE KEBABS

Kebabs and biryani are among my favorite Indian dishes. I just have one serious problem with restaurant kebabs—the price. You pay $7 to $10 for one measly little kebab and I always want more. This recipe makes a lot of kebabs for the price of one pound of meat, and it's absolutely as delicious as the best restaurant kebabs I've ever had— and let me assure you, I've had quite a few in my life. I like to serve these on a naan, with some yogurt or raita, thinly sliced red onions, and a bit of fresh cilantro on top. **SERVINGS: 4**

PREP TIME: 10 MINUTES

STANDING TIME: 30 MINUTES

COOK TIME: 15 MINUTES

TOTAL TIME: 55 MINUTES

COOK TEMPERATURE:
350°F/400°F

DIETARY CONSIDERATIONS:
GRAIN-FREE, GLUTEN-FREE,
EGG-FREE, NUT-FREE,
SOY-FREE, DAIRY-FREE,
PALEO, LOW-CARB

1 **pound ground lamb**

½ **cup finely minced onion**

¼ **cup chopped fresh mint**

¼ **cup chopped fresh cilantro**

1 **tablespoon minced garlic**

½ **teaspoon ground turmeric**

½ **teaspoon cayenne pepper**

¼ **teaspoon ground cardamom**

¼ **teaspoon ground cinnamon**

1 **teaspoon kosher salt**

1. In the bowl of a stand mixer fitted with the paddle attachment, combine the lamb, onion, mint, cilantro, garlic, turmeric, cayenne, cardamom, cinnamon, and salt. Mix on low speed until you have a sticky mess of spiced meat. If you have time, let the mixture stand at room temperature for 30 minutes (or cover and refrigerate for up to a day or two, until you're ready to make the kebabs).

2. Divide the meat into eight equal portions. Form each into a long sausage shape. Place the kebabs in a single layer in the air-fryer basket. Set the air fryer to 350°F for 10 minutes. Increase the air-fryer temperature to 400°F and cook for 3 to 4 minutes more to brown the kebabs. Use a meat thermometer to ensure the kebabs have reached an internal temperature of 160°F (medium).

VIETNAMESE GRILLED PORK SAUSAGES (NEM NUONG)

Your best bet for these is to choose a fatty ground pork. Although your air fryer will help render much of the fat out of the sausage as it cooks, you want to start with lots of fat for its flavor. I often serve this with store-bought sweet chili sauce and some cut cucumbers and call it a day. Either way, it's utterly yummy. **SERVINGS: 4**

PREP TIME: 30 MINUTES

CHILL TIME: 30 MINUTES

COOK TIME: 15 MINUTES

TOTAL TIME: 1 HOUR 15 MINUTES

COOK TEMPERATURE: 375°F

DIETARY CONSIDERATIONS: GLUTEN-FREE, EGG-FREE, NUT-FREE, SOY-FREE, DAIRY-FREE

For the Sausages

- 1 heaping tablespoon jasmine rice
- 2 tablespoons fish sauce
- 2 garlic cloves, minced
- 1 tablespoon sugar
- ½ teaspoon black pepper
- ½ teaspoon kosher salt
- ½ teaspoon baking powder
- 1 pound finely ground pork

For Serving

Hot cooked rice or rice noodles

Shredded lettuce

Fresh mint and basil leaves

Sliced cucumber

Sliced scallions

Dipping Sauce

1. **For the sausages:** Place the rice in a small heavy-bottomed skillet. Toast over medium heat, stirring continuously, until it turns a deep golden yellow color, 5 to 8 minutes. Pour the rice onto a plate to cool completely. Grind in a spice or coffee grinder to a fine powder.

2. In a large bowl, stir together the rice powder, fish sauce, garlic, sugar, pepper, salt, and baking powder until thoroughly combined. Add the pork and mix gently until the seasonings are incorporated.

3. Divide the meat mixture into eight equal pieces. Roll each into a 3-inch-long log. Cover lightly with plastic wrap. Refrigerate for at least 30 minutes or up to 24 hours.

4. Arrange the sausages in the air-fryer basket. Set the air fryer to 375°F for 15 minutes. Use a meat thermometer to ensure the sausages have reached an internal temperature of 160°F.

5. Arrange the sausages, lettuce, mint, basil, cucumbers, and scallions over the rice. Serve with the dipping sauce.

Dipping Sauce (Nuoc Cham): Thinly slice 3 fresh Thai bird chiles (or 1 serrano chile) on an angle. Set aside one-third of the chiles. In a mortar, combine the chiles; 1 garlic clove, sliced; and 3 tablespoons sugar. Pound to a paste. Transfer to a small bowl. Add ⅔ cup warm water, 5 tablespoons fish sauce, 2 tablespoons finely shredded carrot, 1½ tablespoons fresh lime juice, and the reserved chile slices. Let stand for 10 minutes before serving.

ITALIAN SAUSAGE & CHEESE MEATBALLS

PREP TIME: 10 MINUTES

COOK TIME: 20 MINUTES

TOTAL TIME: 30 MINUTES

COOK TEMPERATURE: 350°F

DIETARY CONSIDERATIONS:
GRAIN-FREE, GLUTEN-FREE,
EGG-FREE, NUT-FREE,
SOY-FREE, LOW-CARB

I created this recipe years ago when I started to eat a ketogenic diet. These are simple little snackers that reheat quite well. I used to make a batch and keep them in the fridge for a quick bite when I got hungry. They are so good, though, that they disappear quite quickly. There's just something about sausage and cheese together that makes them irresistible. **SERVINGS: 4**

- ½ **pound bulk Italian sausage**
- ½ **pound 85% lean ground beef**
- ½ **cup shredded sharp cheddar cheese**
- ½ **teaspoon onion powder**
- ½ **teaspoon garlic powder**
- ½ **teaspoon black pepper**

1. In a large bowl, gently mix the sausage, ground beef, cheese, onion powder, garlic powder, and pepper until well combined.

2. Form the mixture into 16 meatballs. Place the meatballs in a single layer in the air-fryer basket. Set the air fryer to 350°F for 20 minutes, turning the meatballs halfway through the cooking time. Use a meat thermometer to ensure the meatballs have reached an internal temperature of 160°F (medium).

SWEDISH MEATBALLS

This recipe came to me from a friend whose family is Swedish, so you know these meatballs are authentic. Before that, I used to rely on the frozen ones from that certain Swedish mega-store—not any more! **SERVINGS: 4**

PREP TIME: 25 MINUTES

COOK TIME: 20 MINUTES

TOTAL TIME: 45 MINUTES

COOK TEMPERATURE: 350°F

DIETARY CONSIDERATIONS: NUT-FREE, SOY-FREE

For the Meatballs

- ¾ cup fresh bread crumbs
- ¼ cup heavy cream
- ¼ cup finely chopped onion
- ½ teaspoon dried parsley flakes
- ½ teaspoon kosher salt
- ¼ teaspoon ground allspice
- ¼ teaspoon freshly grated nutmeg
- ¼ teaspoon white pepper
- ½ pound 85% lean ground beef
- ½ pound ground pork
- 1 large egg, beaten
- 1 egg white, lightly beaten

For the Gravy

- 2 tablespoons salted butter
- 2 tablespoons all-purpose flour
- 1½ cups low-sodium beef broth
- 1 teaspoon Worcestershire sauce
- ¼ cup heavy cream

  Kosher salt and black pepper

For Serving

  Chopped fresh parsley

  Lingonberry jam

1. **For the meatballs:** In a large bowl, mix the bread crumbs and cream until well combined; let stand for 5 minutes. Add the onion, parsley flakes, salt, allspice, nutmeg, and white pepper. Stir to make a thick paste. Add the ground beef, ground pork, egg, and egg white. Mix until evenly combined.

2. Form into 1-inch meatballs. Place in a single layer in the air-fryer basket. Set the air fryer to 350°F for 20 minutes, turning halfway through the cooking time.

3. **Meanwhile, for the gravy:** In a medium saucepan, melt the butter over medium heat. Add the flour and cook, whisking, until smooth. Whisk in the broth and Worcestershire. Bring to a simmer. Add the cream. Reduce the heat to medium-low and simmer until the gravy thickens, about 10 minutes. Season with salt and black pepper.

4. At the end of the cooking time, use a meat thermometer to ensure the meatballs have reached an internal temperature of 160°F (medium).

5. Transfer the meatballs to a serving bowl. Ladle the gravy over the meatballs and sprinkle with parsley. Serve with lingonberry jam.

KHEEMA MEAT LOAF

Yup, another recipe I created because I'm a variety junkie. I like regular meat loaf just fine, but I love kheema meat loaf. (Kheema means ground meat, but implicit in that simple term is a host of flavors, from cardamom and cloves, to turmeric and cayenne, as the word is also used to describe this richly spiced dish). I have a friend who bought herself an extra freezer to freeze large batches of my Instant Pot kheema recipe. When she got herself an air fryer, I decided to make this for her, and it was a big hit. This meat loaf is just different enough to add variety, but approachable enough that everyone will enjoy it. It also makes great sandwiches the next day.

SERVINGS: 4

PREP TIME: 10 MINUTES

COOK TIME: 15 MINUTES

STANDING TIME: 5 MINUTES

TOTAL TIME: 30 MINUTES

COOK TEMPERATURE: 350°F

DIETARY CONSIDERATIONS: GRAIN-FREE, GLUTEN-FREE, NUT-FREE, SOY-FREE, DAIRY-FREE, PALEO, LOW-CARB

- 1 pound 85% lean ground beef
- 2 large eggs, lightly beaten
- 1 cup diced yellow onion
- ¼ cup chopped fresh cilantro
- 1 tablespoon minced fresh ginger
- 1 tablespoon minced garlic
- 2 teaspoons Garam Masala (page 181)
- 1 teaspoon kosher salt
- 1 teaspoon ground turmeric
- 1 teaspoon cayenne pepper
- ½ teaspoon ground cinnamon
- ⅛ teaspoon ground cardamom

1. In a large bowl, gently mix the ground beef, eggs, onion, cilantro, ginger, garlic, garam masala, salt, turmeric, cayenne, cinnamon, and cardamom until thoroughly combined.

2. Place the seasoned meat in a 7-inch round baking pan with 4-inch sides. Place the pan in the air-fryer basket. Set the air fryer to 350°F for 15 minutes. Use a meat thermometer to ensure the meat loaf has reached an internal temperature of 160°F (medium).

3. Drain the fat and liquid from the pan and let stand for 5 minutes before slicing.

4. Slice and serve hot.

LEBANESE KOFTA KEBABS

It's all about the spice mix in these koftas, so be sure to grind the spices fresh just as you are about to cook. This is another one of those recipes that requires very little hands-on time and can be made in advance and reheated. Just be sure to undercook the kebabs a little if you plan to reheat them. **SERVINGS: 4**

PREP TIME: 10 MINUTES

STANDING TIME: 30 MINUTES

COOK TIME: 10 MINUTES

TOTAL TIME: 50 MINUTES

COOK TEMPERATURE: 350°F

DIETARY CONSIDERATIONS: GRAIN-FREE, GLUTEN-FREE, SOY-FREE, EGG-FREE, NUT-FREE, DAIRY-FREE, LOW-CARB

1 pound 85% lean ground beef (see Note)

¼ cup chopped fresh parsley, plus more for garnish

2 tablespoons Kofta Kebab Spice Mix (page 182)

1 tablespoon vegetable oil

1 tablespoon minced garlic

1 teaspoon kosher salt

1. In the bowl of a stand mixer fitted with the paddle attachment, combine the ground beef, parsley, spice mix, vegetable oil, garlic, and salt. Mix on low speed until you have a sticky mess of spiced meat. If you have time, let the mixture stand at room temperature for 30 minutes (or cover and refrigerate for up to a day or two, until you're ready to make the kebabs).

2. Divide the meat into four equal portions. Form each into a long sausage shape. Place the kebabs in a single layer in the air-fryer basket. Set the air fryer to 350°F for 10 minutes. Use a meat thermometer to ensure the kebabs have reached an internal temperature of 160°F (medium).

3. Transfer the kebabs to a serving platter. Sprinkle with additional parsley and serve.

NOTE:

★ I used ground beef, but you can use any kind of meat you'd like, including ground chicken, ground lamb, or a combination of beef and lamb—which would be fabulous. If you use leaner ground meat such as venison, bison, or turkey, you may need to add a little more oil and cook the kebabs until they're just done, being very careful to not overcook them.

CHEESY LOW-CARB LASAGNA

Can it be a lasagna if it doesn't have pasta? Does a low-carb lasagna have to have noodles or veggies? In all honesty, I don't love zucchini in my low-carb lasagna, so I decided to do away with the veggies and the pasta, and just use the elements of a lasagna that have the most flavor—the meat, cheese, and sauce. You could certainly add back the veggies if you want, but try it this way first and see if it isn't more of a flavor bomb for you. **SERVINGS: 4**

PREP TIME: 10 MINUTES

COOK TIME: 10 MINUTES

TOTAL TIME: 20 MINUTES

COOK TEMPERATURE: 375°F

DIETARY CONSIDERATIONS:
GRAIN-FREE, GLUTEN-FREE,
NUT-FREE, SOY-FREE,
LOW-CARB

For the Meat Layer

Extra-virgin olive oil

1 pound 85% lean ground beef

1 cup prepared marinara sauce

¼ cup diced celery

¼ cup diced red onion

½ teaspoon minced garlic

Kosher salt and black pepper

For the Cheese Layer

8 ounces ricotta cheese

1 cup shredded mozzarella cheese

½ cup grated Parmesan cheese

2 large eggs

1 teaspoon dried Italian seasoning, crushed

½ teaspoon each minced garlic, garlic powder, and black pepper

1. **For the meat layer:** Grease a 7½-inch barrel cake pan (see Note, page 11) with 1 teaspoon olive oil.

2. In a large bowl, combine the ground beef, marinara, celery, onion, garlic, salt, and pepper. Place the seasoned meat in the pan.

3. Place the pan in the air-fryer basket. Set the air fryer to 375°F for 10 minutes.

4. **Meanwhile, for the cheese layer:** In a medium bowl, combine the ricotta, half the mozzarella, the Parmesan, lightly beaten eggs, Italian seasoning, minced garlic, garlic powder, and pepper. Stir until well blended.

5. At the end of the cooking time, spread the cheese mixture over the meat mixture. Sprinkle with the remaining ½ cup mozzarella. Set the air fryer to 375°F for 10 minutes, or until the cheese is browned and bubbling.

6. At the end of the cooking time, use a meat thermometer to ensure the meat has reached an internal temperature of 160°F.

7. Drain the fat and liquid from the pan. Let stand for 5 minutes before serving.

VIETNAMESE "SHAKING" BEEF (BO LUC LAC)

This French-inspired Vietnamese dish is bound to be a hit. I usually use it as part of a salad so I don't have to make two separate things for dinner. A simple squirt of lime juice, with some salt and pepper added to the salad, is all your need for a dressing. **SERVINGS: 4**

PREP TIME: 20 MINUTES

MARINATING TIME: 30 MINUTES

COOK TIME: 4 MINUTES PER BATCH

TOTAL TIME: 1 HOUR

COOK TEMPERATURE: 400°F

DIETARY CONSIDERATIONS: EGG-FREE, NUT-FREE, DAIRY-FREE

For the Meat

- 4 garlic cloves, minced
- 2 teaspoons soy sauce
- 2 teaspoons sugar
- 1 teaspoon toasted sesame oil
- 1 teaspoon kosher salt
- ¼ teaspoon black pepper
- 1½ pounds flat iron or top sirloin steak, cut into 1-inch cubes

For the Salad

- 2 tablespoons rice vinegar or apple cider vinegar
- 2 tablespoons vegetable oil
- 1 garlic clove, minced
- 2 teaspoons sugar
- ¼ teaspoon kosher salt
- ¼ teaspoon black pepper
- ½ red onion, halved and very thinly sliced

- 1 head Bibb lettuce, leaves separated and torn into large pieces
- ½ cup halved grape tomatoes
- ¼ cup fresh mint leaves

For Serving

Lime wedges

Coarse salt and freshly cracked black pepper

1. **For the meat:** In a small bowl, combine the garlic, soy sauce, sugar, sesame oil, salt, and pepper. Place the meat in a gallon-size resealable plastic bag. Pour the marinade over the meat. Seal and place the bag in a large bowl. Marinate for 30 minutes, or cover and refrigerate for up to 24 hours.

2. Place half the meat in the air-fryer basket. Set the air fryer to 450°F for 4 minutes, shaking the basket to redistribute the meat halfway through the cooking time. Transfer the meat to a plate (it should be medium-rare—still pink in the middle). Cover lightly with aluminum foil. Repeat to cook the remaining meat.

3. **Meanwhile, for the salad:** In a large bowl, whisk together the vinegar, vegetable oil, garlic, sugar, salt, and pepper. Add the onion. Stir to combine. Add the lettuce, tomatoes, and mint and toss to combine. Arrange the salad on a serving platter.

4. Arrange the cooked meat over the salad. Drizzle any accumulated juices from the plate over the meat. Serve with lime wedges, coarse salt, and cracked black pepper.

VIETNAMESE GRILLED PORK (THIT NUONG)

Every time we go to a Vietnamese restaurant, what I really want is the bun thit nuong. That crispy, slightly sweet pork, the peanuts, the cucumbers! Most restaurants give you lots of noodles and not so much meat. Which is yummy, but I always want more of the meat, so I decided to make my own. Serve with the classic accompaniments of rice noodles, cilantro, julienned carrot, and cucumber sticks—or whatever sounds good to you that day! **SERVINGS: 6**

PREP TIME: 10 MINUTES

MARINATING TIME:
30 MINUTES

COOK TIME: 20 MINUTES

TOTAL TIME: 1 HOUR

TEMPERATURE: 400°F

DIETARY CONSIDERATIONS:
EGG-FREE, DAIRY-FREE

¼ cup minced yellow onion

2 tablespoons sugar

2 tablespoons vegetable oil

1 tablespoon minced garlic

1 tablespoon fish sauce

1 tablespoon minced fresh lemongrass

2 teaspoons dark soy sauce

½ teaspoon black pepper

1½ pounds boneless pork shoulder, cut into ½-inch-thick slices

¼ cup chopped salted roasted peanuts

2 tablespoons chopped fresh cilantro or parsley

1. In a large bowl, combine the onion, sugar, vegetable oil, garlic, fish sauce, lemongrass, soy sauce, and pepper. Add the pork and toss to coat. Marinate at room temperature for 30 minutes, or cover and refrigerate for up to 24 hours.

2. Arrange the pork slices in the air-fryer basket; discard the marinade. Set the air fryer to 400°F for 20 minutes, turning the pork halfway through the cooking time.

3. Transfer the pork to a serving platter. Sprinkle with the peanuts and cilantro and serve.

SICHUAN CUMIN LAMB

The closest Sichuan restaurant is an hour away from my house. I love Sichuan lamb, but it's not often I can drive two hours round trip just to indulge my taste buds. This is an easy, hands-off, authentic recipe that is perfect for your air fryer. Do try to get Sichuan peppercorns if you can—they create a tingly numbness on your tongue that's a unique and lovely sensation. **SERVINGS: 4**

PREP TIME: 15 MINUTES

MARINATING TIME:
30 MINUTES

COOK TIME: 10 MINUTES

TOTAL TIME: 55 MINUTES

COOK TEMPERATURE: 350°F

DIETARY CONSIDERATIONS:
EGG-FREE, NUT-FREE,
DAIRY-FREE, LOW-CARB

For the Lamb

- 2 tablespoons cumin seeds
- 1 teaspoon Sichuan peppercorns, or ½ teaspoon cayenne pepper
- 1 pound lamb (preferably shoulder), cut into ½ by 2-inch pieces
- 2 tablespoons vegetable oil
- 1 tablespoon light soy sauce
- 1 tablespoon minced garlic
- 2 fresh red chiles, chopped
- 1 teaspoon kosher salt
- ¼ teaspoon sugar

For Serving

- 2 scallions, chopped
- Large handful of chopped fresh cilantro

1. **For the lamb:** In a dry skillet, toast the cumin seeds and Sichuan peppercorns (if using) over medium heat, stirring frequently, until fragrant, 1 to 2 minutes. Remove from the heat and let cool. Use a mortar and pestle to coarsely grind the toasted spices.

2. Use a fork to pierce the lamb pieces to allow the marinade to penetrate better. In a large bowl or resealable plastic bag, combine the toasted spices, vegetable oil, soy sauce, garlic, chiles, salt, and sugar. Add the lamb to the bag. Seal and massage to coat. Marinate at room temperature for 30 minutes.

3. Place the lamb in a single layer in the air-fryer basket. Set the air fryer to 350°F for 10 minutes. Use a meat thermometer to ensure the lamb has reached an internal temperature of 145°F (medium-rare).

4. Transfer the lamb to a serving bowl. Stir in the scallions and cilantro and serve.

SPICY LAMB SIRLOIN CHOPS

PREP TIME: 10 MINUTES

MARINATING TIME:
30 MINUTES

COOK TIME: 15 MINUTES

TOTAL TIME: 55 MINUTES

COOK TEMPERATURE: 325°F

DIETARY CONSIDERATIONS:
GRAIN-FREE, GLUTEN-FREE,
EGG-FREE, NUT-FREE,
SOY-FREE, DAIRY-FREE,
PALEO, LOW-CARB

Until I made this dish, I hadn't had lamb sirloin chops. Truth be told, I bought them because it was cheaper than the other packages of lamb and I wasn't sure if my recipe was going to work. Turns out, it's a lovely cut, marbled with just the right amount of fat to make air-frying a dream. If you can't find this cut, feel free to substitute a different fatty cut of lamb, but use a meat thermometer to accurately gauge its doneness. **SERVINGS: 4**

½   **yellow onion, coarsely chopped**

4   **coin-size slices peeled fresh ginger**

5   **garlic cloves**

1   **teaspoon Garam Masala (page 181)**

1   **teaspoon ground fennel**

1   **teaspoon ground cinnamon**

1   **teaspoon ground turmeric**

½ to 1   **teaspoon cayenne pepper**

½   **teaspoon ground cardamom**

1   **teaspoon kosher salt**

1   **pound lamb sirloin chops (see headnote)**

1. In a blender, combine the onion, ginger, garlic, garam masala, fennel, cinnamon, turmeric, cayenne, cardamom, and salt. Pulse until the onion is finely minced and the mixture forms a thick paste, 3 to 4 minutes.

2. Place the lamb chops in a large bowl. Slash the meat and fat with a sharp knife several times to allow the marinade to penetrate better. Add the spice paste to the bowl and toss the lamb to coat. Marinate at room temperature for 30 minutes or cover and refrigerate for up to 24 hours.

3. Place the lamb chops in a single layer in the air-fryer basket. Set the air fryer to 325°F for 15 minutes, turning the chops halfway through the cooking time. Use a meat thermometer to ensure the lamb has reached an internal temperature of 145°F (medium-rare).

FILIPINO CRISPY PORK BELLY (LECHON KAWALI)

PREP TIME: 10 MINUTES

COOK TIME: 15 MINUTES

STANDING TIME: 20 MINUTES

TOTAL TIME: 45 MINUTES

COOK TEMPERATURE: 400°F

DIETARY CONSIDERATIONS:
EGG-FREE, NUT-FREE,
DAIRY-FREE, LOW-CARB

I made this pork belly three different ways—stovetop, oven broiler, and air fryer—to see which was best. The air fryer won on two counts. One, I didn't have to stand over it and babysit it. But two, I got a much crispier end result than with any other method. Easier and better—what's not to like?   **SERVINGS: 4**

1   pound pork belly

3   cups water

6   garlic cloves

2   tablespoons soy sauce

1   teaspoon kosher salt

1   teaspoon black pepper

2   bay leaves

1. Cut the pork belly into three thick chunks so it will cook more evenly.

2. Place the pork, water, garlic, soy sauce, salt, pepper, and bay leaves in the inner pot of an Instant Pot or other electric pressure cooker. Seal and cook at high pressure for 15 minutes. Let the pressure release naturally for 10 minutes, then manually release the remaining pressure. (If you do not have a pressure cooker, place all the ingredients in a large saucepan. Cover and cook over low heat until a knife can be easily inserted into the skin side of pork belly, about 1 hour.) Using tongs, very carefully transfer the meat to a wire rack over a rimmed baking sheet to drain and dry for 10 minutes.

3. Cut each chunk of pork belly into two long slices. Arrange the slices in the air-fryer basket. Set the air fryer to 400°F for 15 minutes, or until the fat has crisped.

4. Serve immediately.

TACO CHILE CASSEROLE

This takes the best of tacos and chiles rellenos and combines them into an easy, tasty casserole. All the taste, none of the fuss. There's really not a lot to this very easy-to-make dish. **SERVINGS: 4**

PREP TIME: 10 MINUTES

COOK TIME: 15 MINUTES

TOTAL TIME: 25 MINUTES

COOK TEMPERATURE: 350°F

DIETARY CONSIDERATIONS: NUT-FREE, SOY-FREE, LOW-CARB

For the Ground Beef

- 1 pound 85% lean ground beef
- 1 tablespoon salt-free taco seasoning
- 1 teaspoon kosher salt
  Vegetable oil spray

For the Topping

- 2 large eggs
- ½ cup milk
- 2 tablespoons all-purpose flour
- 1 (7-ounce) can diced mild green chiles
- 1 cup shredded Mexican cheese blend
- ½ teaspoon kosher salt

1. **For the ground beef:** In a large bowl, combine the beef, taco seasoning, and salt. Mix well.

2. Grease an 7-inch round baking pan (see Note) with vegetable oil spray. Place the seasoned ground beef in the pan.

3. **For the topping:** In a large bowl, whisk together the eggs, milk, and flour until no lumps remain. Fold in the chiles and cheese until well combined. Pour the topping over the ground beef mixture.

4. Place the pan in the air-fryer basket. Set the air fryer to 350°F for 15 minutes. Use a meat thermometer to ensure the meat has reached an internal temperature of 160°F.

5. Drain the fat and liquid from the pan. Let stand for 5 minutes before slicing.

NOTE:

★ This recipe was written to be made in an air fryer with a capacity of 5.3 quarts or more. If your fryer is smaller than that, cut the ingredient quantities in half and cook the casserole in a 6-inch round cake pan with 4-inch sides. You could also make this in a springform pan so that you can unmold the sides and serve the casserole on a plate for a more dramatic presentation.

TURKISH PIZZA (LAHMACUN)

PREP TIME: 20 MINUTES

COOK TIME: 10 MINUTES

TOTAL TIME: 30 MINUTES

COOK TEMPERATURE: 400°F

DIETARY CONSIDERATIONS:
EGG-FREE, NUT-FREE,
SOY-FREE, DAIRY-FREE

Yet another creative and tasty dish with ground beef. When making these pizzas, be sure to use a thin layer of ground meat, but make sure it extends to the very edge of your tortilla, since the meat shrinks a bit and pulls away from the sides as it cooks. Serve these either plain or with a little Tzatziki (page 188) for dipping.   **SERVINGS: 4**

- 4 ounces ground lamb or 85% lean ground beef
- ¼ cup finely chopped green bell pepper
- ¼ cup chopped fresh parsley
- 1 small plum tomato, seeded and finely chopped
- 2 tablespoons finely chopped yellow onion

- 1 garlic clove, minced
- 2 teaspoons tomato paste
- ¼ teaspoon sweet paprika
- ¼ teaspoon ground cumin
- ⅛ to ¼ teaspoon red pepper flakes
- ⅛ teaspoon ground allspice
- ⅛ teaspoon kosher salt

- ⅛ teaspoon black pepper
- 4 (6-inch) flour tortillas

For Serving

Chopped fresh mint

Extra-virgin olive oil

Lemon wedges

1. In a medium bowl, gently mix the ground lamb, bell pepper, parsley, chopped tomato, onion, garlic, tomato paste, paprika, cumin, red pepper flakes, allspice, salt, and black pepper until well combined.

2. Divide the meat mixture evenly among the tortillas, spreading it all the way to the edge of each tortilla.

3. Place 1 tortilla in the air-fryer basket. Set the air fryer to 400°F for 10 minutes, or until the meat topping has browned and the edge of the tortilla is golden. Transfer to a plate and repeat to cook the remaining tortillas.

4. Serve the pizzas warm, topped with chopped fresh mint and a drizzle of extra-virgin olive oil and with lemon wedges alongside.

BEEF, PORK & LAMB

DESSERTS

5-INGREDIENT BROWNIES

I'm never sure whether to call these brownies, or cake, or just chocolate deliciousness. But I know I can always count on them to be easy and delicious. I always think I'll have a few left over, but I never, ever do. They are dangerously easy to put together and absolutely lovely to eat.   **SERVINGS: 6**

PREP TIME: 10 MINUTES

COOK TIME: 25 MINUTES

COOLING TIME: 30 MINUTES

TOTAL TIME: 1 HOUR
5 MINUTES

COOK TEMPERATURE: 350°F

DIETARY CONSIDERATIONS:
GRAIN-FREE, GLUTEN-FREE,
NUT-FREE, SOY-FREE,
VEGETARIAN

Vegetable oil

½ **cup (1 stick) unsalted butter**

½ **cup chocolate chips**

3 **large eggs**

½ **cup sugar**

1 **teaspoon pure vanilla extract**

1. Generously grease a 7-inch square baking pan with vegetable oil.

2. In a microwave-safe bowl, combine the butter and chocolate chips. Microwave on high for 1 minute. Stir very well. (You want the heat from the butter and chocolate to melt the remaining clumps. If you microwave until everything melts, the chocolate will be overcooked. If necessary, microwave for an additional 10 seconds—but stir well before you try that.)

3. In a medium bowl, combine the eggs, sugar, and vanilla. Whisk until light and frothy. While whisking continuously, slowly pour in the melted chocolate in a thin stream and whisk until everything is incorporated.

4. Pour the batter into the prepared pan. Set the pan in the air-fryer basket. Set the air fryer to 350°F for 25 minutes, or until a toothpick inserted into the center comes out clean.

5. Let cool in the pan on a wire rack for 30 minutes before cutting into squares.

ALMOND SHORTBREAD

I used to make a lovely shortbread when my older son was little. There was just one problem—the recipe made a huge panful, and we would eat every last bit of it. Making a smaller but equally delicious portion in the air fryer keeps me safe from my sweet tooth, and also cooks up a lot faster than the traditional recipe.   **SERVINGS: 8**

PREP TIME: 10 MINUTES

COOK TIME: 12 MINUTES

COOLING TIME: 30 MINUTES

TOTAL TIME: 52 MINUTES

COOK TEMPERATURE: 375°F

DIETARY CONSIDERATIONS: EGG-FREE, SOY-FREE, VEGETARIAN

½ cup (1 stick) unsalted butter

½ cup sugar

1 teaspoon pure almond extract

1 cup all-purpose flour

1. In bowl of a stand mixer fitted with the paddle attachment, beat the butter and sugar on medium speed until light and fluffy, 3 to 4 minutes. Add the almond extract and beat until combined, about 30 seconds. Turn the mixer to low. Add the flour a little at a time and beat for about 2 minutes more until well-incorporated.

2. Pat the dough into an even layer in a 7-inch round baking pan. Place the pan in the air-fryer basket. Set the air fryer to 375°F for 12 minutes.

3. Carefully remove the pan from air fryer basket. While the shortbread is still warm and soft, cut it into 8 wedges.

4. Let cool in the pan on a wire rack for 5 minutes. Remove the wedges from the pan and let cool completely on the rack before serving.

GLUTEN-FREE CHICKPEA BROWNIES

What a clever way to sneak some beans into your unsuspecting family! As the mother of a picky eater, I'm always on the lookout for ways to get him to eat better. The fact that this is gluten-free, easy, and delicious is just an added bonus. Don't worry, they don't taste like chickpeas—they taste like brownies. Great, chocolaty brownies. #trusturvashi. **SERVINGS: 6**

PREP TIME: 10 MINUTES

COOK TIME: 20 MINUTES

COOLING TIME: 30 MINUTES

TOTAL TIME: 1 HOUR

COOK TEMPERATURE: 325°F

DIETARY CONSIDERATIONS: GRAIN-FREE, GLUTEN-FREE, NUT-FREE, SOY-FREE, DAIRY-FREE, VEGETARIAN

Vegetable oil

1 (15-ounce) can chickpeas, drained and rinsed

4 large eggs

⅓ cup coconut oil, melted

⅓ cup honey

3 tablespoons unsweetened cocoa powder

1 tablespoon espresso powder (optional)

1 teaspoon baking powder

1 teaspoon baking soda

½ cup chocolate chips

1. Generously grease a 7-inch square baking pan with 4-inch sides with vegetable oil.

2. In a blender or food processor, combine the chickpeas, eggs, coconut oil, honey, cocoa powder, espresso powder (if using), baking powder, and baking soda. Blend or process until smooth. Transfer to the prepared pan and stir in the chocolate chips by hand.

3. Set the pan in the air-fryer basket. Set the air fryer to 325°F for 20 minutes, or until a toothpick inserted into the center comes out clean.

4. Let cool in the pan on a wire rack for 30 minutes before cutting into squares.

EGGLESS FARINA CAKE

Okay, this one took me three tries. My first attempt was absolutely gorgeous—and about as hard as a rock. But if you follow the directions carefully and don't take shortcuts or substitute other ingredients, you'll have an amazing dessert to serve. Check the center of the cake carefully to ensure it's cooked through; if it's not, turn the temperature down to 300°F and give it some more time, since air fryers do vary a little bit in how they cook thicker cakes and quiches.

SERVINGS: 6

PREP TIME: 30 MINUTES (INCLUDES 20 MINUTES STANDING TIME)

COOK TIME: 25 MINUTES

COOLING TIME: 30 MINUTES

TOTAL TIME: 1 HOUR 25 MINUTES

COOK TEMPERATURE: 325°F

DIETARY CONSIDERATIONS: EGG-FREE, NUT-FREE, SOY-FREE, VEGETARIAN

Vegetable oil

2 cups hot water

1 cup chopped dried fruit, such as apricots, golden raisins, figs, and/or dates

1 cup farina (or very fine semolina)

1 cup milk

1 cup sugar

¼ cup ghee (page 187), butter, or coconut oil, melted

2 tablespoons plain Greek yogurt or sour cream

1 teaspoon ground cardamom

1 teaspoon baking powder

½ teaspoon baking soda

Whipped cream, for serving

1. Grease a 7-inch round baking pan with 4-inch sides with vegetable oil.

2. In a small bowl, combine the hot water and dried fruit; set aside for 20 minutes to plump the fruit.

3. Meanwhile, in a large bowl, whisk together the farina, milk, sugar, ghee, yogurt, and cardamom. Let stand for 20 minutes to allow the farina to soften and absorb some of the liquid.

4. Drain the dried fruit and gently stir it into the batter. Add the baking powder and baking soda and stir until thoroughly combined.

5. Pour the batter into the prepared pan. Set the pan in the air-fryer basket. Set the air fryer to 325°F for 25 minutes, or until a toothpick inserted into the center of the cake comes out clean.

6. Let the cake cool in the pan on a wire rack for 10 minutes. Remove the cake from the pan and let cool on the rack for 20 minutes before slicing.

7. Slice and serve topped with whipped cream.

GLUTEN-FREE CHOCOLATE CAKE

I have a very simple criterion for low-carb or gluten-free cakes—they need to taste as good as or better than the real thing. I've made too many cakes that are "good for you" but taste exactly like sawdust. This is not one of those. I would trade it for overly sugary, processed cake any day of the week. As easy as it is to make, I have to be careful not to make it every day of the week! **SERVINGS: 4**

PREP TIME: 10 MINUTES

COOK TIME: 55 MINUTES

COOLING TIME: 30 MINUTES

TOTAL TIME: 1 HOUR 35 MINUTES

COOK TEMPERATURE: 325°F

DIETARY CONSIDERATIONS: GRAIN-FREE, GLUTEN-FREE, SOY-FREE, VEGETARIAN

Unsalted butter, at room temperature

3 large eggs

1 cup almond flour

⅔ cup sugar

⅓ cup heavy cream

¼ cup coconut oil, melted

¼ cup unsweetened cocoa powder

1 teaspoon baking powder

¼ cup chopped walnuts

1. Generously butter a 7-inch round baking pan. Line the bottom of the pan with parchment paper cut to fit.

2. In a large bowl, combine the eggs, almond flour, sugar, cream, coconut oil, cocoa powder, and baking powder. Beat with a hand mixer on medium speed until well blended and fluffy. (This will keep the cake from being too dense, as almond flour cakes can sometimes be.) Fold in the walnuts.

3. Pour the batter into the prepared pan. Cover the pan tightly with aluminum foil. Set the pan in the air-fryer basket. Set the air fryer to 325°F for 45 minutes. Remove the foil and cook for 10 to 15 minutes more, until a knife (do not use a toothpick) inserted into the center of the cake comes out clean.

4. Let the cake cool in the pan on a wire rack for 10 minutes. Remove the cake from the pan and let cool on the rack for 20 minutes before slicing.

5. Slice and serve.

GLUTEN-FREE COCONUT-CHOCOLATE CAKE

PREP TIME: 10 MINUTES

COOK TIME: 55 MINUTES

COOLING TIME: 30 MINUTES

TOTAL TIME: 1 HOUR
35 MINUTES

COOK TEMPERATURE: 325°F

DIETARY CONSIDERATIONS:
GRAIN-FREE, GLUTEN-FREE,
NUT-FREE, SOY-FREE,
VEGETARIAN

The toasted coconut on top of this cake is well worth the few extra minutes it takes to toast, so don't skip it. I use coconut flour in this recipe so that even people who are allergic to almonds can enjoy a dense, moist cake. Do not swap in almond flour for coconut flour in any recipe, though—the two cook up entirely differently. **SERVINGS: 6**

4 tablespoons (½ stick) unsalted butter, melted, plus room-temperature butter for greasing

½ cup sugar

3 large eggs

½ cup heavy cream

1 teaspoon pure vanilla extract

¼ cup coconut flour

2 tablespoons unsweetened cocoa powder

1 teaspoon baking powder

¼ teaspoon kosher salt

3 tablespoons shredded toasted coconut

1 Generously butter a 7-inch round baking pan. Line the bottom of the pan with parchment paper cut to fit.

2. In a large bowl, stir together the melted butter and sugar. Add the eggs, cream, and vanilla. Beat with a hand mixer on medium speed until the ingredients are well blended, 2 to 3 minutes.

3. Add the coconut flour, cocoa powder, baking powder, and salt. Beat on low speed until the ingredients are well combined and the batter is relatively smooth.

4. Pour the batter into the prepared pan. Cover the pan tightly with aluminum foil. Set the pan in the air-fryer basket. Set the air fryer to 325°F for 45 minutes. Remove the foil and cook for 10 to 15 minutes more, until a knife (do not use a toothpick) inserted into the center of the cake comes out clean.

5. Let the cake cool in the pan on a wire rack for 10 minutes. Remove the cake from the pan and let cool on the rack for 20 minutes before slicing.

6. Slice and serve topped with the toasted coconut.

GLUTEN-FREE RICOTTA LEMON POPPY SEED CAKE

PREP TIME: 10 MINUTES

COOK TIME: 55 MINUTES

COOLING TIME: 25 MINUTES

TOTAL TIME: 1 HOUR
30 MINUTES

COOK TEMPERATURE: 325°F

DIETARY CONSIDERATIONS:
GRAIN-FREE, GLUTEN-FREE,
SOY-FREE, VEGETARIAN

The key to baking cakes in an air fryer is to cover with them foil for most of the cooking time, then to remove the foil toward the end to let the top of the cake to brown. This allows the center to cook well, without letting the top burn.   **SERVINGS: 4**

Unsalted butter, at room temperature

1   cup almond flour

½   cup sugar

3   large eggs

¼   cup heavy cream

¼   cup full-fat ricotta cheese

¼   cup coconut oil, melted

2   tablespoons poppy seeds

1   teaspoon baking powder

1   teaspoon pure lemon extract

Grated zest and juice of 1 lemon, plus more zest for garnish

1. Generously butter a 7-inch round baking pan. Line the bottom of the pan with parchment paper cut to fit.

2. In a large bowl, combine the almond flour, sugar, eggs, cream, ricotta, coconut oil, poppy seeds, baking powder, lemon extract, lemon zest, and lemon juice. Beat with a hand mixer on medium speed until well blended and fluffy.

3. Pour the batter into the prepared pan. Cover the pan tightly with aluminum foil. Set the pan in the air-fryer basket. Set the air fryer to 325°F for 45 minutes. Remove the foil and cook for 10 to 15 minutes more, until a knife (do not use a toothpick) inserted into the center of the cake comes out clean.

4. Let the cake cool in the pan on a wire rack for 10 minutes. Remove the cake from pan and let it cool on the rack for 15 minutes before slicing.

5. Top with additional lemon zest, slice and serve.

GLUTEN-FREE SPICE COOKIES

The best part about blogging is the people you get to meet (or e-meet) along the way. My friend Sherlyn had a spice cookie recipe that caught my attention. She allowed me to mess around with her recipe, changing up the ingredients, simplifying the steps—and before we knew it, we had cookies that my son can't stop eating. These are so good! You must try them.   **SERVINGS: 4**

PREP TIME: 10 MINUTES

COOK TIME: 12 MINUTES

COOLING TIME: 20 MINUTES

TOTAL TIME: 35 MINUTES

COOK TEMPERATURE: 325°F

DIETARY CONSIDERATIONS:
GRAIN-FREE, GLUTEN-FREE,
SOY-FREE, VEGETARIAN

4 tablespoons (½ stick) unsalted butter, at room temperature

2 tablespoons agave nectar

1 large egg

2 tablespoons water

2½ cups almond flour

½ cup sugar

2 teaspoons ground ginger

1 teaspoon ground cinnamon

½ teaspoon freshly grated nutmeg

1 teaspoon baking soda

¼ teaspoon kosher salt

1. Line the bottom of the air-fryer basket with parchment paper cut to fit.

2. In a large bowl using a hand mixer, beat together the butter, agave, egg, and water on medium speed until light and fluffy.

3. Add the almond flour, sugar, ginger, cinnamon, nutmeg, baking soda, and salt. Beat on low speed until well combined.

4. Roll the dough into 2-tablespoon balls and arrange them on the parchment paper in the basket. (They don't really spread too much, but try to leave a little room between them.) Set the air fryer to 325°F for 12 minutes, or until the tops of cookies are lightly browned.

5. Transfer to a wire rack and let cool completely. Store in an air-tight container for up to a week.

BAKED SPICED APPLES

This is a great, stupid-simple dessert that you can start when everyone sits down to dinner—and serve hot when they're done. Since it's just fruit, you can tell yourself it's perfectly good for you—until you cover it with ice cream and whipped cream, at which point it's also perfectly good for your taste buds.   **SERVINGS: 4**

PREP TIME: 5 MINUTES

COOK TIME: 10 MINUTES

TOTAL TIME: 15 MINUTES

COOK TEMPERATURE: 350°F

DIETARY CONSIDERATIONS: GRAIN-FREE, GLUTEN-FREE, EGG-FREE, NUT-FREE, SOY-FREE, VEGETARIAN

4   small apples, cored and cut in half (see Note)

2   tablespoons salted butter or coconut oil, melted

2   tablespoons sugar

1   teaspoon apple pie spice

    Ice cream, heavy cream, or whipped cream, for serving

1. Place the apples in a large bowl. Drizzle with the melted butter and sprinkle with the sugar and apple pie spice. Use your hands to toss, ensuring the apples are evenly coated.

2. Place the apples in the air-fryer basket. Set the air fryer to 350°F for 10 minutes. Pierce the apples with a fork to ensure they are tender.

3. Serve with ice cream, or top with a splash of heavy cream or a spoonful of whipped cream.

VARIATIONS TO TRY:

★ Substitute ½ teaspoon each ground cinnamon and ground ginger for the apple pie spice.
★ Add ¼ teaspoon ground cumin to the apple pie spice before sprinkling it on the apples.
★ Substitute ½ teaspoon finely grated orange zest, ½ teaspoon ground ginger, and ¼ teaspoon dried thyme for the apple pie spice.
★ Cover each apple half with a slice of cheddar cheese for the last 2 minutes of cooking.
★ Sprinkle with chopped crystallized ginger right before serving.

NOTE:

★ Some apple varieties are better for cooking than others because they hold their shape when exposed to heat. Good varieties for this recipe include Granny Smith, Fuji, Braeburn, Honeycrisp, Jonathan, Jonagold, Rome Beauty, and Winesap.

CINNAMON-SUGAR ALMONDS

PREP TIME: 5 MINUTES

COOK TIME: 8 MINUTES

TOTAL TIME: 15 MINUTES

COOK TEMPERATURE: 300°F

DIETARY CONSIDERATIONS:
GRAIN-FREE, GLUTEN-FREE,
EGG-FREE, SOY-FREE,
VEGETARIAN

Not only are these easy to make, but they will fragrance your house with a wonderful aroma. Make this base recipe once, then swap in your favorite spices to add some variety. Most traditional spiced nut recipes call for egg whites, but honestly, I never know what to do with the leftover egg yolks, so I tried these with butter instead and it worked really well.   SERVINGS: 4

1   cup whole almonds

2   tablespoons salted butter, melted

1   tablespoon sugar

½   teaspoon ground cinnamon

1. In a medium bowl, combine the almonds, butter, sugar, and cinnamon. Mix well to ensure all the almonds are coated with the spiced butter.

2. Transfer the almonds to the air-fryer basket and shake so they are in a single layer. Set the air fryer to 300°F for 8 minutes, stirring the almonds halfway through the cooking time.

3. Let cool completely before serving.

VARIATIONS TO TRY:

★ Substitute ½ teaspoon ground cumin for the cinnamon.
★ Substitute 2 teaspoons minced fresh rosemary and ⅛ teaspoon cayenne pepper for the cinnamon.

ZUCCHINI NUT MUFFINS

I love being able to make these little bites of happiness, perfect for brunch or a snack. I am also a sneaky mom, so I love being able to sneak some vegetables into a dish that appears decadent—but may actually be good for everyone. **SERVINGS: 4**

PREP TIME: 15 MINUTES

COOK TIME: 15 MINUTES

COOLING TIME: 20 MINUTES

TOTAL TIME: 50 MINUTES

COOK TEMPERATURE: 325°F

DIETARY CONSIDERATIONS: SOY-FREE, DAIRY-FREE, VEGETARIAN

¼ cup vegetable oil, plus more for greasing

¾ cup all-purpose flour

¾ teaspoon ground cinnamon

¼ teaspoon kosher salt

¼ teaspoon baking soda

¼ teaspoon baking powder

2 large eggs

½ cup sugar

½ cup grated zucchini

¼ cup chopped walnuts

1. Generously grease four 4-ounce ramekins or a 7-inch round baking pan with vegetable oil.

2. In a medium bowl, sift together the flour, cinnamon, salt, baking soda, and baking powder.

3. In a separate medium bowl, beat together the eggs, sugar, and vegetable oil. Add the dry ingredients to the wet ingredients. Add the zucchini and nuts and stir gently until well combined. Transfer the batter to the prepared ramekins or baking pan.

4. Place the ramekins or pan in the air-fryer basket. Set the air fryer to 325°F for 15 minutes, or until a cake tester or toothpick inserted into the center comes out clean. If it doesn't, cook for 3 to 5 minutes more and test again.

5. Let cool in the ramekins or pan on a wire rack for 10 minutes. Carefully remove from the ramekins or pan and let cool completely on the rack before serving.

ORANGE-ANISE-GINGER SKILLET COOKIE

This super-flavorful cookie does have a few more ingredients than I usually use, but I couldn't think of which ones to delete without affecting the flavor. If you don't have aniseeds, you can either omit them altogether or substitute a little ground star anise or ground fennel.   **SERVINGS: 2 TO 4**

PREP TIME: 20 MINUTES

COOK TIME: 15 MINUTES

COOLING TIME: 20 MINUTES

TOTAL TIME: 55 MINUTES

COOK TEMPERATURE: 325°F

DIETARY CONSIDERATIONS: NUT-FREE, SOY-FREE, VEGETARIAN

For the Cookie

Vegetable oil

1   cup plus 2 tablespoons all-purpose flour

1   tablespoon grated orange zest

1   teaspoon ground ginger

1   teaspoon aniseeds, crushed

¼   teaspoon kosher salt

4   tablespoons (½ stick) unsalted butter, at room temperature

½   cup granulated sugar, plus more for sprinkling

3   tablespoons dark molasses

1   large egg

For the Icing

½   cup confectioners' sugar

2 to 3   teaspoons milk

1. **For the cookie:** Generously grease a 7-inch round baking pan with vegetable oil.

2. In a medium bowl, whisk together the flour, orange zest, ginger, aniseeds, and salt.

3. In a medium bowl using a hand mixer, beat the butter and sugar on medium-high speed until well combined, about 2 minutes. Add the molasses and egg and beat until light in color, about 2 minutes. Add the flour mixture and mix on low until just combined. Use a rubber spatula to scrape the dough into the prepared pan, spreading it to the edges and smoothing the top. Sprinkle with sugar.

4. Place the pan in the basket. Set the air fryer to 325°F for 15 minutes, or until sides are browned but the center is still quite soft.

5. Let cool in the pan on a wire rack for 15 minutes. Turn the cookie out of the pan onto the rack.

6. **For the icing:** Whisk together the sugar and 2 teaspoons of milk. Add 1 teaspoon milk if needed for the desired consistency. Spread, or drizzle onto the cookie.

NOTE:

★ In testing, some air fryers did better with this recipe when we covered the top with aluminum foil and baked the cookie for 20 minutes, then removed the foil and baked for 10 minutes more. If the results aren't to your liking, try the foil method.

DESSERTS

CARDAMOM CUSTARD

Slow and steady does the job with these custards. Cover them with aluminum foil to keep them from bubbling vigorously. Take my advice—chill them. So much better! Chilling makes them thick and silky-smooth. I cooked these with and without a water bath and found no difference in the texture, so in this recipe, I've called for cooking the ramekins straight in the wire basket. If your air-fryer basket is deep, you could try doubling the recipe and stacking another two ramekins on top as well. **SERVINGS: 2**

PREP TIME: 10 MINUTES

COOK TIME: 25 MINUTES

COOLING TIME: 5 MINUTES

TOTAL TIME: 40 MINUTES

COOK TEMPERATURE: 350°F

DIETARY CONSIDERATIONS:
GRAIN-FREE, GLUTEN-FREE,
NUT-FREE, SOY-FREE,
VEGETARIAN

1 cup whole milk

1 large egg

2 tablespoons plus 1 teaspoon sugar

¼ teaspoon vanilla bean paste or pure vanilla extract

¼ teaspoon ground cardamom, plus more for sprinkling

1. In a medium bowl, beat together the milk, egg, sugar, vanilla, and cardamom.

2. Place two 8-ounce ramekins in the air-fryer basket. Divide the mixture between the ramekins. Sprinkle lightly with cardamom. Cover each ramekin tightly with aluminum foil. Set the air fryer to 350°F for 25 minutes, or until a toothpick inserted in the center comes out clean.

3. Let the custards cool on a wire rack for 5 to 10 minutes.

4. Serve warm, or refrigerate until cold and serve chilled.

MIXED BERRY CRUMBLE

Get yourself a bag of frozen mixed berries and this dessert becomes simplicity itself. The cornstarch helps thicken up the filling and produces a fruit mixture that will have you swearing off ready-made pie fillings. **SERVINGS: 4**

PREP TIME: 10 MINUTES

COOK TIME: 15 MINUTES

COOLING TIME: 5 MINUTES

TOTAL TIME: 30 MINUTES

COOK TEMPERATURE: 400°F

DIETARY CONSIDERATIONS: EGG-FREE, NUT-FREE, SOY-FREE, VEGETARIAN

For the Filling

- 2 cups mixed berries, thawed if frozen
- 2 tablespoons sugar
- 1 tablespoon cornstarch
- 1 tablespoon fresh lemon juice

For the Topping

- ¼ cup all-purpose flour
- ¼ cup rolled oats
- 1 tablespoon sugar
- 2 tablespoons cold unsalted butter, cut into small cubes

  Whipped cream or ice cream (optional)

1. **For the filling:** In a 7-inch round baking pan, gently mix the berries, sugar, cornstarch, and lemon juice until thoroughly combined.

2. **For the topping:** In a small bowl, combine the flour, oats, and sugar. Using two knives or your fingers, cut the butter into the flour mixture until the mixture has the consistency of bread crumbs.

3. Sprinkle the topping over the berries.

4. Place the pan in the air-fryer basket. Set the air fryer to 400°F for 15 minutes. Let cool for 5 minutes on a wire rack.

5. Serve topped with whipped cream or ice cream, if desired.

BAKED BRAZILIAN PINEAPPLE

We have a family tradition of going out to Brazilian churrascarias for Thanksgiving and Christmas. My son Alex is really only interested in three things at these restaurants: filet mignon, pão de quejo (Brazilian cheese bread), and the grilled pineapple, which he can't seem to get enough of. I now make the cheese bread at home for him, but he still craves the pineapple. I know this looks like a stupid-simple recipe. You must try it, though. Air-frying the pineapple with sugar produces a wonderful caramel flavor, enhanced by the cinnamon. Eat plain, or serve with some whipped cream, or vanilla ice cream for a special treat. **SERVINGS: 4**

PREP TIME: 10 MINUTES

COOK TIME: 10 MINUTES

TOTAL TIME: 20 MINUTES

COOK TEMPERATURE: 400°F

DIETARY CONSIDERATIONS: GRAIN-FREE, GLUTEN-FREE, EGG-FREE, NUT-FREE, SOY-FREE, VEGETARIAN

½ cup brown sugar

2 teaspoons ground cinnamon

1 small pineapple, peeled, cored, and cut into spears

3 tablespoons unsalted butter, melted

1. In a small bowl, mix the brown sugar and cinnamon until thoroughly combined.

2. Brush the pineapple spears with the melted butter. Sprinkle the cinnamon-sugar over the spears, pressing lightly to ensure it adheres well.

3. Place the spears in the air-fryer basket in a single layer. (Depending on the size of your air fryer, you may have to do this in batches.) Set the air fryer to 400°F for 10 minutes for the first batch (6 to 8 minutes for the next batch, as the fryer will be preheated). Halfway through the cooking time, brush the spears with butter.

4. The pineapple spears are done when they are heated through and the sugar is bubbling. Serve hot.

SAUCES & SPICE MIXES

CILANTRO PESTO & VARIATIONS

I started a garden this year and . . . So. Much. Cilantro. Which is not a problem for me, since I love cilantro. This sauce is the best way to use cilantro as a seasoning. You can use it as a marinade for raw meat or as a sauce to top cooked meat, although it's perfect with just about anything—grilled meat, samosas, potato patties, and pretty much anything else you can think of. If you hate cilantro, use parsley instead.   **SERVINGS: 4**

PREP TIME: 10 MINUTES

TOTAL TIME: 10 MINUTES

DIETARY CONSIDERATIONS: SUITABLE FOR ALL DIETS

- 1 cup fresh cilantro leaves
- 1 jalapeño
- 2 tablespoons vegetable oil
- 2 tablespoons fresh lemon juice
- 2 tablespoons minced fresh ginger
- 2 tablespoons minced garlic
- 1 teaspoon kosher salt

In a blender, combine the cilantro, jalapeño, vegetable oil, lemon juice, ginger, garlic, and salt. Blend until smooth.

VARIATIONS TO TRY:

★ Add 1 teaspoon Garam Masala (page 181).
★ Add 1 teaspoon each of cumin seeds and coriander seeds.
★ Add 2 tablespoons roasted pistachios.
★ Use ½ cup fresh parsley in place of half the cilantro.
★ Substitute red wine vinegar for the lemon juice.
★ Add 1 teaspoon ras el hanout, ground sumac, or za'atar.

GARAM MASALA

Listen to me—make your own garam masala, make it fresh from whole seeds, and use it up within a month or two. The difference between homemade and store-bought garam masala is night and day. I know it looks like a lot to buy, but my blog and my other cookbooks will show you a hundred different uses for these spices. If you have an Indian grocery store near you, they will carry all of these. If not, try Amazon or other online retailers.

MAKES: 4 TABLESPOONS

PREP TIME: 10 MINUTES

TOTAL TIME: 10 MINUTES

DIETARY CONSIDERATIONS: SUITABLE FOR ALL DIETS

2 tablespoons coriander seeds

1 teaspoon cumin seeds

½ teaspoon whole cloves

½ teaspoon cardamom seeds (from green/white pods)

2 dried bay leaves

3 dried red chiles, or ½ teaspoon cayenne pepper or red pepper flakes

1 (2-inch) piece cinnamon or cassia stick

1 Combine the coriander, cumin, cloves, cardamom, bay leaves, chiles, and cinnamon in a clean coffee or spice grinder. Grind, shaking the grinder lightly so all the seeds and bits get into the blades, until the mixture is broken down to a moderately fine powder.

2. Unplug the grinder and turn it upside down. (You want all the ground spices to collect in the lid so you can easily scoop them out without cutting yourself on the blades.)

3. Transfer the garam masala to an airtight container and store in a cool, dark place for a month or two.

KOFTA KEBAB SPICE MIX

I'm a variety junkie. I love trying new foods, new places, new experiences. But I can always be counted upon to order kofta kebabs at every opportunity. Having this spice mix around makes it a slam dunk to make kofta (page 134) any time you want. **MAKES: 4 TABLESPOONS**

PREP TIME: 10 MINUTES

TOTAL TIME: 10 MINUTES

DIETARY CONSIDERATIONS: SUITABLE FOR ALL DIETS

1 tablespoon coriander seeds

1 tablespoon cumin seeds

1 teaspoon whole black peppercorns

1 teaspoon whole allspice berries

½ teaspoon cardamom seeds (from green/ white pods)

½ teaspoon ground turmeric

1. Combine the coriander, cumin, peppercorns, allspice, cardamom, and turmeric in a clean coffee or spice grinder. Grind, shaking the grinder lightly so all the seeds and bits get into the blades, until the mixture is broken down to the consistency of a fine powder.

2. Unplug the grinder and turn it upside down. (You want all the ground spices to collect in the lid so you can easily scoop them out without cutting yourself on the blades.)

3. Transfer the spice mix to an airtight container and store in a cool, dark place for up to 3 months.

LEBANESE SHAWARMA SPICE MIX

I've used this mix with chicken, with beef, with green beans, with ground beef and rice, with cabbage—there are no limits to how many different ways you can use this fragrant, super-simple mix.

MAKES: 4 TABLESPOONS

PREP TIME: 5 MINUTES

TOTAL TIME: 5 MINUTES

DIETARY CONSIDERATIONS: SUITABLE FOR ALL DIETS

2 teaspoons dried oregano

1 teaspoon ground cinnamon

1 teaspoon ground cumin

1 teaspoon ground coriander

1 teaspoon kosher salt

½ teaspoon ground allspice

½ teaspoon cayenne pepper

In a small bowl, stir together the oregano, cinnamon, cumin, coriander, salt, allspice, and cayenne. Store in an airtight container in a cool, dark place for up to 3 months.

TOMATILLO SALSA

There's nothing better than roasted veggies made into a salsa—but that charred skin can leave a mess on baking sheets and stovetops. Using an air fryer to roast your tomatillos takes away the mess but imparts all the charred flavor you'd get from using the broiler. One note: Add salt to only the portion you intend to use. Without the salt, this sauce lasts in the fridge for up to 10 days. Add salt to all of it, though, and you'll need to eat it up within a few days. Which may not be such a hardship, to be honest.   **SERVINGS: 4**

PREP TIME: 5 MINUTES

COOK TIME: 15 MINUTES

TOTAL TIME: 20 MINUTES

COOK TEMPERATURE: 350°F

DIETARY CONSIDERATIONS: SUITABLE FOR ALL DIETS EXCEPT PALEO

12   tomatillos

2   fresh serrano chiles

1   tablespoon minced garlic

1   cup chopped fresh cilantro leaves

1   tablespoon vegetable oil

1   teaspoon kosher salt

1. Remove and discard the papery husks from the tomatillos and rinse them under warm running water to remove the sticky coating.

2. Place the tomatillos and peppers in a 7-inch round baking pan with 4-inch sides. Place the pan in the air-fryer basket. Set the air fryer to 350°F for 15 minutes.

3. Transfer the tomatillos and peppers to a blender, add the garlic, cilantro, vegetable oil, and salt, and blend until almost smooth. (If not using immediately, omit the salt and add it just before serving.)

4. Serve or store in an airtight container in the refrigerator for up to 10 days.

EASY PEANUT SAUCE

Perfect to use as a salad dressing or satay dipping sauce, for vegetables, or on air-fried tofu or meats.   **SERVINGS: 4**

TOTAL TIME: 5 MINUTES

DIETARY CONSIDERATIONS: EGG-FREE, DAIRY-FREE, VEGAN, VEGETARIAN, LOW-CARB, SOY-FREE

⅓ cup peanut butter

¼ cup hot water

2 tablespoons soy sauce

2 tablespoons rice vinegar

Juice of 1 lime

1 teaspoon minced fresh ginger

1 teaspoon minced garlic

1 teaspoon black pepper

1. In a blender container, combine the peanut butter, hot water, soy sauce, vinegar, lime juice, ginger, garlic, and pepper. Blend until smooth.

2. Use immediately or store in an airtight container in the refrigerator for a week or more.

GOCHUJANG DIP

When my foodie friend John moved away to California, I really missed our never-ending food, work, and life conversations. He came to visit us a few weeks ago and we gushed about our shared love for gochujang (Korean red chile paste). After he left, I put together a few of the things we talked about and came up with this dip. It is so easy to make, and even easier to eat all of, if you're not careful.   **MAKES: A SCANT ½ CUP (4 SERVINGS)**

PREP TIME: 5 MINUTES

TOTAL TIME: 5 MINUTES

DIETARY CONSIDERATIONS: NUT-FREE, DAIRY-FREE, VEGETARIAN

2   tablespoons gochujang (Korean red pepper paste)

1   tablespoon mayonnaise

1   tablespoon toasted sesame oil

1   tablespoon minced fresh ginger

1   tablespoon minced garlic

1   teaspoon agave nectar

1. In a small bowl, combine the gochujang, mayonnaise, sesame oil, ginger, garlic, and agave. Stir until well combined.

2. Use immediately or store in the refrigerator, covered, for up to 3 days.

GHEE

Put the butter in a pot. Heat it. Don't mess with it. Half an hour later, you've got great ghee. No, really—it's that simple. It takes a little bit of practice to know when it's all done, but it's also a very forgiving recipe, so it's hard to go wrong. **MAKES: 2 CUPS**

PREP TIME: 0 MINUTES

COOK TIME: 20 MINUTES

TOTAL TIME: 20 MINUTES

DIETARY CONSIDERATIONS: GRAIN-FREE, GLUTEN-FREE, EGG-FREE, NUT-FREE, SOY-FREE, VEGETARIAN, LOW-CARB, PALEO

1 pound unsalted butter

1. Place the butter in a heavy-bottomed saucepan over medium-low heat. Set a timer for 20 minutes and LEAVE IT ALONE! Don't stir the butter or mess with it in any way. Just let it be. (During this time, the water from the butter will evaporate. You'll see a light foam forming on top of the bubbling butter. It will sound like popcorn popping, but much softer.)

2. At the 20-minute mark, stir the butter and raise the heat to medium-high. Cook, stirring occasionally, until you see the milk solids start to turn brown and settle on the bottom of the pan. If you give up before this stage you are either: a) a quitter, or b) trying to make clarified butter, not ghee.

3. Let the butter cool a little, then strain the clear yellow liquid through a fine-mesh strainer into a jar with a lid. (Discard the brown milk solids.) Seal the jar tightly, and you're done.

4. You can store the ghee on your countertop. As long as you keep the jar sealed and use a clean spoon each time you dig into the ghee, it lasts almost indefinitely.

TZATZIKI

It seems to me that Mediterranean, Middle Eastern, and Indian cuisines all share a version of dishes that combine cooling yogurt with some kind of vegetable. Whether it's an Indian raita, a Persian borani, or a Greek tzatziki, the combination of yogurt, veggies, and a few spices makes a great sauce to accompany all kinds of grilled meats. Traditional tzatziki recipes do not call for tahini. I find, however, that it lends a wonderful nutty, creamy finish that makes this robust sauce perfect for grilled meats.

MAKES: A GENEROUS 2 CUPS (4 SERVINGS)

PREP TIME: 10 MINUTES

TOTAL TIME: 10 MINUTES

DIETARY CONSIDERATIONS:
GRAIN-FREE, GLUTEN-FREE,
EGG-FREE, NUT-FREE,
SOY-FREE, VEGETARIAN,
LOW-CARB

1 large cucumber, peeled and grated (about 2 cups)

1 cup plain Greek yogurt

2 to 3 garlic cloves, minced

1 tablespoon tahini (sesame paste)

1 tablespoon fresh lemon juice

½ teaspoon kosher salt, or to taste

Chopped fresh parsley or dill, for garnish (optional)

1. In a medium bowl, combine the cucumber, yogurt, garlic, tahini, lemon juice, and salt. Stir until well combined. Cover and chill until ready to serve.

2. Right before serving, sprinkle with chopped fresh parsley, if desired.

INDEX

Note: Page references in *italics* indicate photographs.

CHART OF DIETARY CONSIDERATIONS AND COOKING TIMES

RECIPE	PAGE	DAIRY FREE	EGG FREE	GLUTEN FREE	GRAIN FREE	LOW CARB
CHILI-CHEESE TOAST	2		X			
GRILLED CHEESE SANDWICHES	5					
HARD-COOKED EGGS	6	X		X	X	
SCOTCH EGGS	7			X	X	X
SPICY GREEK BAKED FETA WITH HONEY (FETA PSITI)	8		X			
JALAPEÑO POPPER BAKE	11		X	X	X	X
FRESH HERB AND CHEDDAR FRITTATA	12			X	X	X
CHEESE & VEGGIE EGG CUPS	13			X	X	X
PHYLLO-WRAPPED BRIE WITH FIG JAM	14		X			
FRICO (CHEESE CRISPS)	17		X			X
PUFF PASTRY BITES WITH GOAT CHEESE, FIGS & PROSCIUTTO	18					
PANEER TIKKA BITES	20		X	X	X	X
HALLOUMI WITH GREEK SALSA	21		X	X	X	X
BBQ CHICKEN FLATBREADS	22		X			
HOT CRAB DIP	25			X	X	X
CREAM CHEESE WONTONS	26		X			
TART & SPICY INDIAN POTATOES (AMCHOOR POTATOES)	30	X	X	X	X	
CHILES RELLENOS WITH RED CHILE SAUCE	33		X	X	X	
MUSHROOMS & BACON	35	X	X	X	X	X
INDIAN CHINESE CAULIFLOWER (GOBI MANCHURIAN)	36	X	X			X
INDIAN OKRA (BHINDI MASALA)	39	X	X	X	X	X
ROASTED CAULIFLOWER WITH TAHINI	40	X	X	X	X	X
SHAWARMA GREEN BEANS	41	X	X	X	X	X
INDIAN EGGPLANT BHARTA	42	X	X	X	X	X
LEBANESE BABA GHANOUSH	43	X	X	X	X	X
SOUTHWESTERN ROASTED CORN	44		X	X	X	
POTATO FRIES	47	X	X	X	X	
ROOT VEGGIE SHOESTRING FRIES WITH SAFFRON MAYONNAISE	48	X		X	X	
ASIAN TOFU SALAD	50	X	X			X
POTATOES ANNA	51		X	X	X	
WARM SALADE NIÇOISE	52	X		X	X	
AFRICAN PIRI-PIRI CHICKEN DRUMSTICKS	56	X	X	X	X	X
AFRICAN MERGUEZ MEATBALLS	59	X	X	X	X	X
CHICKEN & VEGETABLE FAJITAS	60		X	X	X	X
CHICKEN SHAWARMA	63		X			
COCONUT CHICKEN MEATBALLS	64	X	X			
THAI-STYLE CORNISH GAME HENS (GAI YANG)	65	X	X			
CRISPY CRACKED-PEPPER CHICKEN WINGS	66	X	X			
GOCHUJANG CHICKEN WINGS	69	X				
HAWAIIAN HULI HULI CHICKEN	70	X	X			
PERSIAN CHICKEN KEBABS (JOOJEH KABAB)	73		X	X	X	X
SPICY INDIAN FENNEL CHICKEN	74	X	X	X	X	X
TANDOORI CHICKEN	77		X	X	X	X
THAI CURRY MEATBALLS	78	X	X	X	X	X
TURKISH CHICKEN KEBABS (TAVUK SHISH)	81		X	X	X	X
YELLOW CURRY BAKED CHICKEN	82	X	X	X	X	X
GREEK CHICKEN SOUVLAKI	85		X	X	X	X
STICKY SESAME CHICKEN LEGS	86	X	X			
PECAN CRUSTED CHICKEN TENDERS	88	X		X	X	X
HERBED ROAST CHICKEN BREAST	89		X	X	X	X
PERUVIAN-STYLE CHICKEN WITH GREEN HERB SAUCE	90	X	X	X	X	X
SHRIMP SCAMPI	94		X	X	X	X
TILAPIA ALMONDINE	96		X	X	X	X
DUKKAH-CRUSTED HALIBUT	97	X	X	X	X	X

EVERY DAY EASY AIR FRYER

NUT FREE	PALEO	SOY FREE	VEGETARIAN	VEGAN	30 MINS OR LESS	COOK TIME	TOTAL TIME	TEMPERATURE
X		X	X		X	5	10	325
X		X			X	5	13	350
X	X	X	X		X	25	25	250
X		X				15	35	400
X		X	X		X	10	15	400
X		X			X	15	30	400
X		X	X		X	20	30	300
X		X	X		X	19	30	300/400
X		X	X			15	35	400
X		X	X		X	5	15	375
X		X				10	50	400
X		X	X			10	50	325
X		X	X		X	6	21	375
X		X			X	10	20	400
X		X			X	7	12	400
X		X	X		X	6	16	350
X		X	X	X	X	15	25	400
X		X				20	40	400
X	X	X			X	10	15	375
X			X	X	X	20	30	400
X		X	X	X	X	15	25	375
X		X	X	X	X	20	30	400
X		X	X	X	X	10	15	375
X		X	X	X		20	45	400
X		X	X	X		20	45	400
X		X	X		X	10	20	375
X		X	X	X	X	20	30	400
X	X	X				15	35	400
X			X	X		15	40	400
X		X	X			40	55	400
X		X			X	15	30	400
X	X	X				20	65	400
X		X				10	50	400
X		X				23	40	375
X		X				15	55	350
X					X	14	24	350/400
X						20	65	400
X		X				20	35	400
X						25	40	400
X						15	55	350
X		X				12	52	350/400
X		X				15	55	350
X		X				15	55	350
X	X	X			X	10	20	400
X		X				15	60	375
		X				20	60	375
X		X				15	65	350/400
X					X	20	25	400
	X	X			X	12	17	350
X	X	X				25	40	375
X	X	X				15	60	350
X	X	X			X	8	16	325
	X	X			X	10	20	325
	X	X				10	32	400

NUT FREE	PALEO	SOY FREE	VEGETARIAN	VEGAN	30 MINS OR LESS	COOK TIME	TOTAL TIME	TEMPERATURE
X	X	X				10	50	375
X		X			X	8	18	325
X		X				12	35	300
X					X	12	22	400
X						12	57	400
X		X			X	10	25	375
X		X				15	40	375
X		X			X	8	20	400
X		X			X	8	13	350
X		X			X	10	15	350
X		X			X	15	25	350
X		X				8	48	400
		X				8	48	400
X						15	55	350
X						15	55	400
X						30	70	350
X						15	55	400
X	X	X				15	55	350/400
X		X				15	75	375
X		X			X	20	30	350
X		X				20	45	350
X	X	X			X	15	30	350
X		X				10	50	350
X		X			X	10	20	375
X						8	60	400
						20	60	400
X						10	55	350
X	X	X				15	55	325
X						15	45	400
X		X			X	15	25	350
X		X			X	10	30	400
X		X	X			25	65	350
		X	X			12	52	375
X		X	X			20	60	325
X		X	X			25	85	325
		X	X			55	95	325
X		X	X			55	95	325
		X	X			55	90	325
		X	X			12	35	325
X		X	X		X	10	15	350
		X	X		X	8	15	300
		X	X			15	50	325
X		X	X			15	55	325
X		X	X			25	40	350
X		X	X		X	15	30	400
X		X	X		X	10	20	400
X	X	X	X	X	X		10	
X	X	X	X	X	X		10	
X	X	X	X	X	X		10	
X	X	X	X	X	X		5	
X		X	X	X	X	15	20	350
		X	X	X	X		5	
			X		X		5	
X	X	X	X		X	20	20	
X		X	X		X		10	

Continue Cooking with Urvashi Pitre's

AUTHORIZED BY INSTANT POT®

Instant Pot®
FAST & EASY

100 Simple and Delicious
Recipes for Your Instant Pot

Urvashi Pitre

HMH hmhco.com